GIULIANI: NASTY MAN

by

Edward I. Koch

BARRICADE BOOKS/NEW YORK

Published by Barricade Books Inc.
150 Fifth Avenue
Suite 700
New York, NY 10011

Library of Congress Cataloging-in-Publication Data
Koch, Ed, 1924-
    Giuliani : nasty man / by Edward I. Koch.
      p. cm.
    ISBN 1-56980-155-X
    1. Giuliani, Rudolph W. 2. New York (N.Y.)--Politics and government--1951- 3. Giuliani, Rudolph W.--Psychology. I. Title.
F128.57.G58K63 1999
974.7'1043'092--dc21
                                          99-23689
                                            CIP

Printed in the United States of America.

10 9 8 7 6 5 4 3 2 1

DEDICATION

This book is dedicated to the people of the City of New York, who deserve the best from their elected officials. I have endeavored to point out where the current mayor—Rudolph W. Giuliani—has served them well and where he has failed them. A mayor must be more than a police commissioner. The mayor is the surrogate hand and heart of the city.

PROLOGUE

On November 8, 1977, I was elected New York City's 105th mayor. I served from January 1, 1978 to the end of 1989. I am proud of many of my administration's achievements, but I suspect that history will single out for special recognition my stewardship of New York City through its worst fiscal crisis, which I inherited from my predecessor and which almost bankrupted the city.

Unlike legislators, who often can pick and choose their shots, mayors—like governors and presidents—have to play the hand that is dealt them. And like presidents and governors, big-city mayors often have a limited shelf-life. That too comes with the turf. When day after day you have to decide issues not of your choosing, you inevitably alienate people.

As the years go by and the number of those on the losing side of your decisions grows larger, you pass the peak of your popularity. And, of course, there is the simple issue of longevity. People do get tired of you. I reached the end of my electoral political career in 1989 when—after twenty-six years in party and public office—I lost the Democratic party primary to David Dinkins.

In the general election in 1989, Dinkins ran against Republican Rudolph Giuliani and narrowly won. Prior to his election, David Dinkins had a varied career in city politics, having served as City Clerk and Manhattan Borough President. He became New York

City's first African-American mayor. My verdict on the David Dinkins' years is simple: very nice man, very poor mayor.

In four short years the quality of life in New York City plummeted. Crime rates, especially for violent street crime, shot up dramatically. The Dinkins Administration was overwhelmed by the need to provide shelter for the homeless. Defying heretofore universal mathematical certainties, the city's Off Track Betting Corporation—under a Dinkins-appointed OTB President—actually lost money. The mortal blow to his administration was the three-day pogrom which took place in Crown Heights in August of 1991. To many New Yorkers of a literary bent, the city had become like the famous opening lines of the Yeats' poem "The Second Coming":

> Turning and turning in the widening gyre
> The falcon cannot hear the falconer;
> Things fall apart; the centre cannot hold;
> Mere anarchy is loosed upon the world....

Things seemed to be falling apart. And they were.

With the Crown Heights pogrom as a backdrop, Rudy Giuliani once again ran for mayor. In a November 1993 rematch with David Dinkins, Giuliani was elected New York City's 107th mayor.

During my tenure as mayor, Rudy had been U.S. Attorney of the Southern District of New York and we interacted on several occasions. I had been publicly criticizing the weakness of penalties issued by many state court judges in drug cases, and on one occasion he invited me to address his assistant U.S. attorneys on the subject of drug interdiction.

Rudy responded to my remarks by instituting what became known as Federal Day. One day each month all drug arrests made by the New York City

Police Department in Manhattan and the Bronx were prosecuted in federal rather than state court. Both the penalties and the chances of a successful prosecution are greater in federal court than in the state court, particularly because of different rules of evidence.

The number of drug cases prosecuted by Rudy under this program was insignificant compared to those prosecuted by district attorneys in each of New York City's five boroughs. Nevertheless, I believe that the fear of being tried in federal court and subjected to harsher penalties did have a deterrent effect, and I appreciated Giuliani's involvement.

Before the 1993 election, Giuliani sought my support and invited me to lunch about half a dozen times, seeking to enlist my active participation in his campaign.

David Garth, who had worked on all of my mayoral campaigns, was Rudy's campaign media consultant. David and I were, and are, good friends. When David asked me to participate in Rudy's campaign, I told him that I had several serious concerns about Rudy Giuliani.

I was particularly concerned about Giuliani's ability to be fair. David urged me to raise those concerns with Rudy over lunch, and I did.

During his tenure as U.S. Attorney, Rudy had been involved in an investigation that resulted in the indictment of a number of Wall Street brokers. One of the cases involved charges against three brokers who were arrested and handcuffed and whose pictures made the front page of the papers. The charges were ultimately dismissed against all three. In my judgment, when these brokers were arrested in their offices they were handcuffed in order to demean them before their colleagues.

In another of Rudy's investigations, Sukhreet Gable, the emotionally fragile daughter of New York State Supreme Court Justice Hortense Gable, had secretly tape-recorded her mother for the purposes of criminal prosecution. I was appalled by these actions.

At one of our lunches, I told him: "There are two things that trouble me about you, Rudy. The first is, why did you allow the federal agents to handcuff the stockbrokers in their offices? They weren't dangerous, so why were they humiliated before their colleagues?

"The second is, how you could allow Sukhreet Gabel to tape her mother on the telephone to get evidence to prosecute her criminally?" I then added, "You are perceived as Inspector Javert."

Giuliani responded first by asking who Inspector Javert was. I explained that he was a relentless prosecutor in the book and musical "Les Miserables."

Giuliani then said, "I had nothing to do with [handcuffing the stockbrokers]. It was the agent's decision because the brokers refused to leave, thinking the arrest was a joke."

Giuliani then answered my question about Sukhreet Gable. He claimed that he "told [Sukhreet] not to, but she inadvertently pressed the wrong button and taped her." He went on, "I explained this to the judge at the arraignment."

I wanted to believe him so I made no further inquiry at the time. I no longer believe him.

I had already decided that the city could not survive four more years under Mayor David Dinkins. I was particularly outraged by Dinkins' failure to act during a violent riot that broke out in the Crown Heights section of Brooklyn in August 1991.

Crown Heights had become a neighborhood uneasily shared by blacks and Hasidic Jews. That summer, a car carrying some members of the Lubavitch

Community who were returning from a visit to the grave of the wife of the Grand Rebbe, accidentally struck and killed a black child. In response, black mobs swept through Crown Heights assaulting Lubavitch Jews—who were easily identifiable in their kaftans— and killing a young man, Yankel Rosenbaum. According to the media, those in the mob surrounding Yankel Rosenbaum were shouting, "Jew, Jew, kill the Jew!"

For three long days and nights, David Dinkins failed to order the police action necessary to stop the terror in Crown Heights. At the time, I thought to myself: if there had been a comparable attack on blacks by whites in Harlem when I was mayor, I would have been run out of town.

Because the city seemed like it was on the brink of disintegration, and I believed that Dinkins egregiously mishandled the response to the pogrom in Crown Heights, I decided to endorse Rudy Giuliani and actively participate in his campaign for mayor in 1993.

Other than the candidate himself, four people were most responsible for Giuliani's victory. The first was David Garth, Giuliani's brilliant campaign media consultant who was totally in charge of the campaign.

The second was Ray Harding. Ray was the leader of the Liberal Party, and gave Rudy his party's line on the ballot. This gave Democrats who were unable to bring themselves to vote on the Republican line the ability to cross party lines by voting for Rudy on the Liberal Party line.

The third person who made Giuliani's victory possible was Bobby Wagner (the son of former Mayor, Robert F. Wagner, Jr.) who had served in my administration as a deputy mayor. Bobby made a brilliant TV commercial for Rudy directed at Democrats.

The fourth person was me. New York City is a Democratic town. I remained very popular with the electorate even after having lost the Democratic primary to David Dinkins in 1989. In that primary, I garnered forty-two percent of the vote, and most political observers thought that my imprimatur was essential if Republican candidate Rudy Giuliani was to win.

The people of New York City were wrestling with the same grave doubts about both candidates that I had. Many New Yorkers were distressed that there was no other responsible election option. Indeed, they were so distressed that as I walked around the streets of the city, I would be importuned—sometimes ten to fifteen times a day—by passersby with, "Mayor, you must run again, you must run again."

My response was always the same: "No, the people threw me out and now the people must be punished."

Often their retort was, "Oh, Mayor, we have been punished enough!"

Giuliani was elected by a margin of two percent. In the beginning he played the hand dealt him well. Giuliani had made his name as an organized crime busting, no-nonsense prosecutor. As mayor, his first goal was the reduction of violent street crime, and crime levels did go down.

Although he had the benefit of a reduction in violent crime nationwide, and many experts concluded that the reduction in crime in New York City was due to a demographic age reduction, reduced use of crack cocaine, and mandatory and longer prison sentences, they also attributed the reduction to better and more sophisticated use of police resources.

Giuliani has publicly, and also in my presence, boasted, "I run the Police Department." The *New York Times* reported that Giuliani micro-managed the NYPD, even deciding who would receive detective badges. Such decisions are not generally the province of the mayor (and should not be), but rather that of the Police Commissioner. In the Giuliani Administration, however, the Police Department is very much the mayor's creature.

Giuliani does deserve credit for reducing crime by an even greater percentage than the national average. If crime had gone up he would have been blamed, so since it went down, he has every right to claim credit.

In addition, the homeless, who during Dinkins' term had lived on sidewalks all over Manhattan, became invisible. Moreover, benefitting from an unprecedented economic boom, particularly on Wall Street, which filled the city's coffers, Giuliani spruced up the city. Rudy rode a well-deserved wave of popularity.

I recognized and applauded Rudy's achievements. In 1994, the first year of the Giuliani Administration, I wrote three columns about the mayor: January 2nd, February 18th, and December 16th. These columns were overwhelmingly supportive.

But even during his first year in office, Giuliani's hubris emerged. In my column of December 16th, I leavened praise with a gentle warning: "Take it from me, hubris is every mayor's greatest danger. On balance, Rudy deserves a very high score at the end of his first year. His mettle will be brutally tested in the years to come."

As 1995 unfolded, New Yorkers began to see more and more of the authoritarian side of its 107th mayor. We began to learn that Rudy is not content to prevail; he must destroy his opponents.

People were finding out that you cannot have an honest disagreement with Rudy. If you disagree with him he scorns you as dishonest, stupid, or a hypocrite. We also learned that Rudy believes that he is solely responsible for every single one of his administration's achievements. Apparently, no one else has contributed to them. However, Rudy never accepts responsibility for any failures.

In 1995, Giuliani's second year in office, I wrote three columns about him: February 17th, June 23rd, and October 6th. I criticized the mayor in each of these columns.

In my first column, I criticized his treatment of New York City Police Commissioner William Bratton. Just as Giuliani deserved some of the credit for the drop in crime, so did his able Police Commissioner. But crime reduction was Rudy's beat, and Commissioner Bratton liked the limelight.

Giuliani resented Bratton's being on the cover of Time magazine. The mayor also appeared jealous of Bratton for getting credit for assembling the team and improving the philosophy and techniques in the police department necessary to implement Rudy's "zero tolerance" campaign which led to the huge reductions in crime.

Envious of Bratton's press, Giuliani required that Bratton fire John Miller, his brilliant press secretary. Giuliani also publically berated Bratton for spending too much time at Elaine's, a popular and chic restaurant. Eventually, Giuliani's behavior drove Bratton out of office.

Just as Giuliani could not abide sharing credit with Bratton, the mayor could not tolerate the generally good press received by New York City Schools Chancellor Ramon Cortines. The Chancellor also committed the grievous, unforgivable sin of standing up to Giuliani.

In my second column, I reported that Giuliani could not get New York City Schools Chancellor Ramon Cortines to accept his demand that Cortines fire those on his staff whom Giuliani did not like. Giuliani reacted to Cortines' refusal by publicly demeaning Cortines, referring to him as "precious" and someone who "talks out of both sides of his mouth." Giuliani also said that Cortines "plays this little game of innocent little victim... It's time for him to stop all the whining...grow up...stop playing little victim." Rudy was not nice. But, as we came to learn, his treatment of Cortines was vintage Giuliani.

In my third column, I pointed out that "Rudy Giuliani is no Fiorello LaGuardia. When LaGuardia erred, he was capable of saying, 'When I make a mistake, it's a beaut.' Rudy cannot admit error."

Jews are a politically potent part of the New York City electorate. In October 1995, Rudy decided to pander to ultra-religious (fundamentalist) Jewish New Yorkers. In the process, he committed a major violation of common decency and protocol. Giuliani stood on the stage at Lincoln Center and imperiously ordered Palestinian Authority Chairman Yasir Arafat to leave the theater where Arafat was attending a function jointly sponsored by the City of New York and the United Nations.

This outrageous public discourtesy was broadcast around the world. It undoubtedly resulted in millions of people feeling sympathetic towards Arafat, and contemptuous of the mayor and New York City. Giuliani was seen as pandering to Arafat's most fanatical opponents, believing that in doing so he was helping his own political fortunes.

I am a fiercely proud Jew who supports Israel with fervor and passion. Nevertheless, I only felt ashamed that Giuliani had disgraced our city—and his office—with his discourtesy to an invitee of the United Nations.

In 1996, I wrote seven columns about the mayor. This was a significant increase over previous years. Every one of these columns was negative. My major break with Giuliani came in January, 1996 when he gutted the merit judicial selection system that I created at the beginning of my first term as mayor, and which had been in effect for sixteen years, through the term of David Dinkins.

Judges should be selected on the basis of merit, not politics. Once appointed, judges must be insulated from political pressure. Although it limited my power as mayor, I created a selection and reappointment system based on merit.

I created this system by voluntarily relinquishing the mayor's unilateral authority (i.e., without confirmation of any legislative body) to appoint criminal and family court judges, and to make interim appointments to the civil court. I also agreed to—without exception—abide by the judgments of the Mayor's Judiciary Committee and the New York City Bar Association on whether or not a judge whose term had expired should be re-appointed.

Giuliani reasserted the mayor's right to overrule the Committees, and in fact did on several occasions. The Executive Director of the Fund for Modern Courts warned that Giuliani's decision "may very well have a chilling effect on judges." It certainly did.

In each of my subsequent columns about Giuliani's performance as mayor, I pointed out how his actions and decisions were hurting the city as well as himself. In my last column of that year, I announced that I would not support him in his bid for re-election: "Why? Because Rudy Giuliani has failed as our mayor."

In 1997, a mayoral election year, I wrote four columns about Giuliani, three of which were negative. In that election, we had another terrible choice. I could not vote for the Democratic candidate for mayor, Ruth Messinger, because I believed that she represented the radical left wing of the Democratic party. Instead, I crossed party lines and, despite my very strong reservations, voted to reelect Giuliani. But because of those reservations, I would not endorse him.

When I was asked what the difference was between voting and endorsing, I said that I believed you must vote, even if for the lesser of two evils, but I could not advise others for whom they should vote in such a situation. In my July 18th, 1997 column I wrote, "Will I weep if Giuliani is reelected, or be joyous if Messinger wins? Neither. New York City will survive either scenario."

As the number of outrageous acts committed by Giuliani began to escalate, so did the number of my columns about him.

In 1998, I wrote fourteen negative columns about Giuliani. His authoritarian personality, high-handed style of governing, and vindictiveness became ever more apparent.

This was the year Giuliani horrendously transformed the environment at City Hall. He ordered it surrounded by barbed wire and concrete barricades, ostensibly to protect the building and those who worked there from terrorist attack. Interestingly, federal authorities in New York City and Washington D.C. did not believe such extraordinary measures were necessary to protect their buildings.

In my December 11th column, I wrote of City Hall, "The entire building has been placed virtually off limits to the public, even though it is the seat of New York City government. Imagine if Congress closed the Capitol to visitors; something it has never done despite bombings and shootings."

In this column I also remarked that I could only speculate as to why Giuliani decided to remove the official portraits of myself and David Dinkins from the Blue Room at City Hall. I suggested that Giuliani might have found the faces of his two mayoral critics on the walls of the Blue Room more disconcerting than I could imagine.

The nastiness of Giuliani's personality was revealed time and time again. He demeaned everyone who either questioned or criticized him. His method of governing had been reduced to a campaign of demonizing and trivializing anyone who opposed him.

I was not alone in calling the Mayor to task. Respected reporters and columnists in New York City mocked the Mayor.

In February of 1998, Mark Krieger of the *New York Daily News* wrote, "Mayor Needs First Lesson in Civility." Krieger reported on Giuliani's attacks on other public officials. He reported that with respect to New York State's highly respected Comptroller Carl McCall, Giuliani carped, "He really has no credibility." On David Dinkins, Krieger wrote that "Just a couple of weeks ago, Giuliani said: 'If I had [David Dinkins's] record I'd be kind of embarrassed to show my face.'"

Krieger also reported Giuliani's campaign to denigrate New York City Board of Education President Carol Gresser. Krieger wrote, "But Giuliani still had Carol Gresser to kick around. Giuliani didn't like her interfering when he tried to pick a new chancellor, even if it was not really his job to choose one. 'She might as well take her silly remarks and do something else with them,' Giuliani said. As for his talks with would-be chancellors, Giuliani added that they are 'beyond Carol Gresser's ability to carry on a substantive discussion.'"

Clyde Haberman of the *New York Times* also pointed out Giuliani's mean-spiritedness. In his October 2, 1998 column, Haberman criticized Giuliani for referring to White House Drug Czar General Barry McCaffrey—who was the most highly decorated and youngest four-star General in the Army when he retired—as "a disaster."

What prompted Giuliani's savage attack? In response to Giuliani's statement that methadone treatment was immoral and would no longer be used in New York City's drug treatment clinics, General McCaffrey defended the use of methadone for treating heroin addicts. Giuliani later rescinded his decision to cease methadone treatment.

In 1998 Giuliani began focusing police resources on jaywalking. The NYPD began giving jaywalkers summonses, and the city built barriers to block pedestrians from crossing the street at certain corners in Manhattan.

In December, 1998, Bill Hutchinson of the *New York Daily News* wrote "Hizzoner's Still Wheel Menace, Sez Report." This story focused on Giuliani's own history of breaking traffic laws, which was particularly relevant because of Giuliani's crusade against jaywalkers. When questioned about his police-driven GMC Suburban doing seventy-five miles per hour in a fifty miles per hour zone and committing several other moving violations, a brusque Giuliani scoffed at the reporter saying: "Report that to the Police Department, and we'll have it adjudicated in court. Thank you."

Finally, the year 1999, which started off with a series of political controversies.

In January Giuliani announced a plan to start exporting the city's garbage to other states.

Even the *New York Post*, which editorially adores Giuliani and often lionizes him as if he is the mayor who can do no wrong, criticized the mayor's plan in an editorial on January 15, 1999. "Gotham's garbage problem cannot be solved exclusively by exportation, which is [Giuliani's] current plan. Giuliani would do well to acknowledge that. Instead, he has made an argument for exportation that it's hard to believe he actually believes: 'People in Virginia like to utilize New York City because we're a cultural center... We don't have the room to handle the garbage that's produced not just by New Yorkers, but by the three million more people that come here that utilize the place every day.'"

When Virginia's Governor James C. Gilmore 3rd defended his state from becoming the repository of New York City's garbage, Giuliani accused him of being "some politician trying to get on television."

In February, Giuliani announced that he was moving the New York City Campaign Finance Board from a leased space in Manhattan to a city-owned building in Brooklyn.

Giuliani alleged that the reason for the move was to save money. Not true.

The move actually would not save a nickel because the city had leased the office space in Manhattan until the year 2010, with an option to terminate in 2005.

Furthermore, the Manhattan location was modified to accommodate the board's computer system, whereas the city-owned building in Brooklyn was not.

Because of the city's obligation under this lease, another city agency would have to be placed in the space anyway, and the city would have to pay to modify the city-owned space in Brooklyn. Moving the board would cost, rather than save the city money.

Why the mayor's wrath?

The Board had fined Giuliani's campaign $242,930 for violating campaign laws during the 1997 election—the highest penalty for exceeding contribution limits in New York City history. In addition, the Board had disagreed with Giuliani's interpretation of the Campaign Financing Law.

According to Bruce Lambert's article in the *New York Times*, Giuliani also threatened to cut off the Campaign Finance Board's operational budget. "We'll probably hold up their money, hold back their money, because it's illegal," the mayor warned. The mayor then accused the Board of "stubbornness and arrogance" and "the height of intellectual dishonesty."

All because the universally respected Father Joseph O'Hare, the New York City Campaign Finance Board's Chairman, a Jesuit Priest and President of Fordham University, had the audacity to disagree with the mayor over the amount of matching funds permissible under the law.

Bob Herbert of the *New York Times* also devoted several columns to Giuliani's modus operandi. In one of these columns, Herbert pointed out that under former administrations, there was a notion that "City Hall was a place that belongs to you, a place where you might be welcome. It was once, but that's over. Rudolph Giuliani is the mayor now. City Hall belongs to him and the changed atmosphere reflects his personality—cold and remote and unforgiving."

By February 1999, I had already written four columns about Giuliani.

In my column of February 26th, I urged Hillary Clinton to run for the Senate, writing, "If she runs, Hillary—like Bobby Kennedy—will be attacked as an outsider. But she will be a breath of fresh air. It takes a state to elect a senator."

In an earlier column, I pointed out that Giuliani acts like a petty tyrant, and wrote that "he will seek to destroy an opponent, as perhaps he might have pulled the wings off a fly as a child."

However, all of Giuliani's comments and actions paled in significance to the firestorm that erupted over a number of incidents of police brutality over the past several years.

The fires began to smolder in 1994 with the death of Anthony Baez, who died as the result of a police officer using an illegal choke hold on him. Baez suffered from asthma, adding to his vulnerability.

Although deeply grateful for the reduction in street crime and still overwhelmingly supportive of the NYPD, significant segments of the public were becoming uneasy about the methods some officers used to enforce the law.

The smoldering coals burst into flame with the apparent torture of Abner Louima, a Haitian immigrant, in 1997. Louima was allegedly sodomized with a toilet plunger by police officers and otherwise tortured while in the precinct house.

Finally, the flames spread into a full-fledged conflagration with the Amadou Diallo tragedy. Diallo, an unarmed immigrant from Guinea, was shot at forty-one times by four undercover police officers while he was standing in the vestibule of his apartment building. Nineteen of these shots struck Diallo, and he died at the scene.

The officers were members of the NYPD's elite Street Crime Unit, whose slogan is "We Own The Night." Apparently Diallo fit the description of a rape suspect the officers were looking for. This case has become a major albatross for Giuliani.

Taken together, these incidents struck a raw nerve in many New Yorkers. The City is anything but homogeneous. New York is, and always has been, America's mosaic. In order for the mosaic to work, the police must enforce the law vigorously but also fairly, legally, and without prejudice.

In each of these three incidents, the officers were white, and the civilians were members of a minority group. It was the mayor's responsibility to support the

vast majority of officers who do their jobs professionally, but also to make clear to the police and the public that racism and brutality will not be tolerated, even
in the name of fighting crime.

Giuliani failed to provide that kind of leadership
and reassurance. Instead of immediately meeting with
minority community leaders to discuss their concerns,
he rebuffed those leaders, treating them as if they
were not worthy of his time.

For example, during an interview with the editorial board of the *Daily News*, Giuliani remarked, in the
paper's words, that "the biggest beef New Yorkers
have with the cops isn't that they're brutal—it's that
they're rude."

In effect, Giuliani's comment denigrated the more
than 1,200 people of all races and religions—including
rabbis, ministers, priests, lawyers, members of congress (including Charles Rangel from New York), former mayor David Dinkins, Jesse Jackson, union leaders, and other concerned citizens—who, in acts of nonviolent civil disobedience, voluntarily got arrested in
order to display their outrage at the Diallo tragedy and
Giuliani's response to it.

Many of those arrested were also there to raise
the level of consciousness of Mayor Giuliani about the
seriousness of the people's rage, and to compel him to
meet with minority community leaders, which he had
declined to do. Eventually, they were successful, and
Giuliani did finally reach out to and meet with some of
those leaders.

Giuliani made his worst comment to date the day
after the four police officers involved in the Diallo
shooting were indicted. Giuliani said the police are
"second-guessed by some of the worst in society." This
is undoubtedly true on many occasions. But was it a
sensible or decent thing to say during the aftermath of

allegations which, if true, constitute one of the most serious instances of police misconduct in New York City history?

Giuliani followed his worst comment with his dumbest. He made this silly comment the day after Justin Volpe, the officer charged with sodomizing Abner Louima, pled guilty to torturing him.

During the trial of Justin Volpe and the other police officers facing criminal charges in connection with the assault on and torture of Mr. Louima, several officers came forward to testify for the prosecution. The testimony of these officers was apparently so credible and devastating that Volpe decided he had no choice but to plead guilty and throw himself on the mercy of the court.

Mayor Giuliani reacted to the officers' willingness to testify in this case saying that it "destroys the myth of the 'blue wall of silence.'"

A truly foolish and insensitive remark. The fact that police officers agreed to tesify against Volpe is an aberration. Perhaps these officers testified because of the truly degenerate act of torture committed, or out of fear they'd be prosecuted for obstruction of justice. After all, there were so many police officers in the precinct house who were aware of what happened.

Or perhaps these officers testified because they were unusually truthful and courageous. In which case, so much the better. In any event, their cooperation in this case does not make the general refusal to testify a myth, which is defined as an unfounded or false notion.

Giuliani's comment is the archetypical insensitive remark of a nasty man.

SOME TIPS FROM ONE WHO'S BEEN THERE

As Rudy Giuliani takes office, he has the support and good will of most New Yorkers. Surely a majority of those who voted against him want his administration to succeed for their own sake and that of the city.

The new mayor will quickly find this support is ephemeral. In 90 days he will be standing alone, winning and losing support issue by issue. The mayor has no permanent partners. His allies will change depending on the issue—and the time of day.

Over the past four years, New York City has been in a free fall. Recently, 42% of New Yorkers polled said they would move out if given a choice. Rudy can help keep them here by being candid, setting realistic goals, and generating energy and excitement.

The mayor can instill confidence by holding town hall meetings in each of the city's communities. In my 12 years I had 135 local meetings. Some were heated, even raucous. For several of the more potentially explosive gatherings, the police assigned to me insisted that I wear a bulletproof vest. I did. The mayor can never cede the streets or any public place to the predators or the rioters. He must never cancel an appearance because of security concerns.

Rudy can improve morale among city employees by regularly meeting with his commissioners and their top 25 people, urging them to express candidly their aspirations and tell him their problems.

The mayor has to know more about city issues than the reporters who will question him daily. If they sense he is not informed or is reluctant to face them, they will react like piranha. Rudy should answer press questions on policy matters himself, not through his press secretary.

While the mayor should take on other elected public officials with vigorous language when required, his press aides should never take it upon themselves to question the motives of those officials. If Rudy feels he has been unfairly criticized, he should try to educate the public with respect to the truth and never allow his silence to be perceived as assent.

Every mayor needs a priority issue. Mine was housing. I suggest Rudy make his the health of the city's children. He should institute a program providing free medical care at city clinics and municipal hospitals for all children, from cradle to first grade, regardless of income eligibility.

Two staff agencies are vital to any mayor's success: The Office of Management and Budget and the Corporation Counsel. OMB guards the treasury and is responsible for keeping the city solvent and using the city's limited resources to best advantage. The Corporation Counsel protects the city from those scheming to rip it off. These departments should be protected from attrition and lay-offs.

The mayor must demonstrate his concern for the police officers and firefighters who are on the front lines every day. His presence at their hospital bedsides when they have been injured in the line of duty means more to them than speeches. When cops are accused of brutality, he should assume they acted professionally unless that presumption is refuted by credible evidence made available to him.

Rudy must be prepared to fire incompetent and corrupt employees expeditiously. The corrupt should be publicly discharged and their crimes referred to law enforcement. The inadequate should be required to resign, but without suffering public disgrace.

There will be those who will seek to divide the city racially by criticizing the mayor's every appointment and action. If he has been fair in his selection process, enthusiastically encouraging the disparate citizens of this city to apply and then picking the best applicant for a particular job, he shouldn't give a second thought to the yammering of those who would use race as a bludgeon to accumulate power.

Mayor Giuliani should never allow racial, ethnic or gender quotas to be used in hiring, purchasing, contracting, or any other city program. He should immediately revoke all prior mayoral executive orders that created such quotas and set-asides. Programs for the poor or for small businesses should never exclude, as his predecessor did, those white males who are disadvantaged economically.

Finally, Rudy should make his first action important and symbolic. He should bring back to the mayor's office the portrait of Fiorello LaGuardia and the desk used by that great mayor, both of which were banished by former Mayor David Dinkins.

THE DAILY NEWS   FEBRUARY 18, 1994

CHALLENGED BY GOD & RADICALS, GUILIANI SHOWS RIGHT STUFF

Rudy Giuliani has been mayor for 49 days. He has been tested, as was I, by both God and the radicals, and he has passed both tests with high marks. Since taking office, Rudy has had to deal with 10 snowstorms, including two major ones just last week.

I can relate to the wrath of God. In mid-January 1978, just weeks after I was inaugurated, we had the largest snowstorm in 100 years. As the snow was falling, and the badgering reporters asked how I was feeling, I looked to heaven and wondered aloud, "When will He send in the locusts?"

Now the radicals. I think I had a little more time than Rudy before they threw down the gauntlet.

But I do recall the Reverend Herbert Daughtry trying to break up my inaugural festivities at the Brooklyn Museum. At the time he was protesting an alleged incident of police brutality that had taken place under the former administration.

One high-ranking public official from Brooklyn stood up and told the crowd we were going to leave because of the disruption. I said no, that we wouldn't be pushed out. I turned to Daughtry and asked, "Why are you doing this? I just got elected. I didn't have anything to do with that police matter." Then I offered to meet with him at City Hall to discuss it. He agreed and left with his entourage.

In Mayor Giuliani's case, even before his inauguration he was informed that the radicals would urge their political supporters and elected officials not to meet with him or shake his hand. Many of these people were those who sought to bring me down. Rudy will find that the cast of characters has changed very little.

Rudy was in office less than two weeks when someone decided to test the cops and Rudy's support of them. A bogus 911 call of a robbery in progress brought cops to a commercial building in Harlem where a Nation of Islam mosque is located on the third floor.

Since the mosque was considered a "sensitive" location, city protocol required that a police supervisor be called to the scene.

Erroneously, the 911 operator did not alert the police brass. But the cops didn't even have an opportunity to test the protocol because they were assaulted in a stairway by members of the Nation of Islam, resulting in injuries to eight cops, with one female cop suffering a broken nose. In addition, a police gun and radio were taken.

As you would expect, the Reverend Al Sharpton was waiting in the wings, demanding to meet with the mayor. Had he witnessed the incident? Was he a member of the Nation of Islam? No and no. He was simply a demagogue looking for trouble.

I had my first go-round with Sharpton relatively early on. In April 1978, Sharpton came to my office with several other ministers and called on me to sign a petition to Congress demanding billions in reparations for descendants of slaves, to be paid by the U.S. Treasury.

I asked him if I could study it and get back to him. He said that unless I signed it then and there, he would sit down in front of my office and not permit any business to be done. I told him he couldn't do that. He and three other ministers sat down in the outer office and refused to leave.

I said to a police officer on the scene, "Remove them."

He said, "What if they resist?"

I replied, "Have you never heard the word arrest?" They were removed and issued summonses. In the ensuing 12 years, no one ever tried to stage a sit-in at my office again.

David Dinkins recently said: "The reason I have not responded to every little comment out there is I want to give the mayor an opportunity to go ahead and be mayor, an opportunity Ed Koch never gave me." Not true. When I left office in 1989, I announced that I would not make any critical comments concerning Dinkins for six months. I kept that promise.

On the other hand, Dinkins, his self-described good guy image notwithstanding, has already criticized Giuliani in just the first six weeks.

When it comes to acts of God and the radicals, the French had a phrase for it: *Plus a change, plus c'est la même chose*—the more things change, the more they stay the same. Whether on the Seine or on the Hudson, it's hard to tell the difference between City Hall and the Hotel de Ville.

RUDY'S FIRST: A REPORT CARD

The mayor's doing nicely on Ed's 12-step program

When Rudy Giuliani took office, I offered him a dozen suggestions in the spirit of "The Twelve Days of Christmas." As his first year in office draws to a close, it seems like the appropriate time to grade the 107th mayor of the City of New York on his performance.

I was graded during my three terms by many critics who could have no conception of what it was like to be mayor. They had never been in charge of 250,000 employees, had never been close to directing the priorities of a $31 billion budget (the fourth largest in the United States), and had never been responsible for the general welfare of 7.5 million people made up of more than 175 different races, ethnic loyalties, and religious persuasions.

The most demanding were—and still are—the media: reporters, columnists, and editorial writers. I make my assessment of the mayor in my capacity as a journalist. I've often said, "It's much more fun being a critic than a victim."

Let me now list the suggestions I made and how the mayor has responded:

1. *Hold regular town hall meetings throughout the city.* Rudy has held 12—very responsible.
2. *Meet with commissioners and their top staffs.* He does so regularly.
3. *Know more about the city issues than the*

reporters covering City Hall. Rudy has proven he can go toe-to-toe with the media.

4. *Respond personally, not through your press secretary, to reporters' questions.* The mayor holds as many press conferences as I did and answers reporters directly every day.

5. *Educate the public and never allow your silence to be perceived as assent.* Rudy has not been silent on any important issue.

6. *Pick a priority issue.* The mayor chose privatization and is actively implementing it.

7. *Make your key agencies the Office of Management and Budget and Corporation Counsel, and your closest advisors the OMB director and Corporation Counsel.* Here, the mayor chose two brilliant men, Abe Lackman and Paul Crotty, and they are part of his inner circle.

8. *Demonstrate your concern for the police officers and fire-fighters who protect this city at risk of their own lives.* The mayor has supported them with fervor.

9. *Fire the incompetent and the corrupt expeditiously.* I'm not aware of any corruption in the Giuliani administration. There are a number of incompetents who should be terminated. I believe Rudy will act on that problem within the next six months, tracking the 18 months it took me to shake up my administration.

10. *Ignore those who would have you select your commissioners on a racial, ethnic, and gender basis.* Pick the best people available. The mayor has done that, despite attacks from those who believe in preferential treatment.

11. *Revoke all prior executive orders creating*

racial, ethnic, and gender quotas. Rudy has started the demolition of reverse-discrimination programs, but there are many still in effect which he should also end.

12. *Bring back to the mayor's office the portrait of Fiorello LaGuardia and his desk, both of which had been removed by Rudy's predecessor.* Rudy did that immediately on taking office. It's nice having the Little Flower looking over your shoulder.

What the mayor needs to learn to do is pick his fights and not get involved in more confrontations than he can handle. He demonstrated courage in taking on the striking Legal Aid attorneys and the illegal street peddlers on 125th Street. But the two current battles the mayor is waging—one with Schools Chancellor Ramon Cortines and the other with Speaker Peter Vallone and the City Council—are alarming.

The mayor's attacks on the chancellor are incessant and unreasonable. Quite correctly, the chancellor is held in high regard by most experts in the field. If Rudy doesn't show support, Cortines may well quit when his contract ends in June. Rudy now has no concept of what racial and ethnic battles can be like, but he'll learn if he gets involved in the process of choosing a successor to Cortines. All of his energy will be sapped in such a fight.

The mayor's other equally needless battle involves his squabbling with Speaker Vallone and the City Council over revisions and reductions in the budget. It was folly on Rudy's part not to accommodate a large portion of the City Council's modest budget restorations, particularly since they are overwhelmingly thoughtful and needed, such as funding for food banks.

The Council, like a great fish in the ocean, wants the sun to shine on its scales several times in the course of a year. Its need for public accolades must occasionally be sated, particularly when restraint has been shown and, especially in this case, when what was called for by the Council was a change of priorities with respect to $90 million of the $800 million budget revisions.

Rudy may win the technical battle in court concerning city charter limits on the Council's power, but he will surely lose the war in June of next year when a new budget is adopted. There the Council will prevail, since it is able to override any mayoral veto.

Take it from me, hubris is every mayor's greatest danger. On balance, Rudy deserves a very high score at the end of his first year. His mettle will be brutally tested in the years to come.

NEW YORK POST   FEBRUARY 17, 1995

RUDY REACHES THE HUBRIS STAGE

What's happening to Rudy Giuliani?

Here he is, 14 months into his term, and he's fighting with everyone. First it was Schools Chancellor Ramon Cortines. Then it was City Council Speaker Peter Vallone. Now it's Police Commissioner William Bratton.

At the outset, I have to make clear that I am one of Rudy's supporters—and I intend to support him in 1997 when he runs again. His achievements in a very short time have been remarkable.

Mayor Giuliani has brought to City Hall a sense of leadership that was missing in the prior four years. He has reached reasonable labor settlements. The productivity measures obtained at the Department Of Sanitation and with the school custodians are extraordinary. The merger of the three police forces and Rudy's ending the Legal Aid strike on his terms were tremendous victories.

Now Rudy has introduced an explosive budget which the *New York Times*, in a four-column, front-page headline, heralded as, "Giuliani Seeks Deepest Cut In City Spending Since 1930's." He may have no alternative—and even so, the mayor says, "New York City would still be providing more money in each of these programs [programs for the poor] than any other city in America..."

While I favor cuts, the mayor's challenge now is to assure New Yorkers that what he's saying is accurate by providing comparison data from other major cities. If he doesn't, this budget will go down in history as a local St. Valentine's Day Massacre.

Rudy's greatest personal challenge during the last mayoral campaign was convincing voters that he was a warmhearted human being to whom New Yorkers could relate, and not simply a prosecutor in the image of Torquemada.

He was fortunate in having as his opponent a mayor who had alienated so many. David Dinkins was seen as having declined to protect Korean merchants in Flatbush from illegal picketing by blacks, and as having failed to protect Jews in Crown Heights from physical assault by a black mob. In short, he was perceived to be more interested in tennis and tuxedos than in the less pleasurable burdens of office.

Since his victory, Rudy has tried desperately to convey in public the warmth that he naturally and easily displays in private. At times, however, it's like watching the body english of Frankenstein's monster. Interesting, but heavy-footed.

Now, Mayor Giuliani has fired a number of individuals who report not to him, but to his commissioners. Attempting to clarify the situation, his very able first deputy mayor, Peter Powers, said: "We've been telling commissioners that a lot of people are off agenda... The mayor's going to stand on his record. People will look at what he promised and what he delivered. We have to have people there who believe in his agenda, his contract with the voters."

According to the *Times*, the dismissals are expected to reach up to 300 this week. Some of those fired worked in prior administrations going back as far as Abe Beame, and including both mine and David Dinkins'.

The people fired were not policy-makers; they carried out policy. They did not subvert Rudy's agenda or Rudy. They responded to their bosses and, as far as I know, no commissioners are engaged in doing Rudy in. Far from it—they want to be there for Giuliani's second term.

There's nothing wrong with the mayor doing a reassessment. I reorganized my government after the first year, firing some people and redeploying others—but it was at the top levels, involving deputy mayors and commissioners. For Rudy to reach down into agencies and tell competent commissioners, like Bill Bratton or Health Commissioner Margaret Hamburg or Environmental Protection Commissioner Marilyn Gelber, whom to fire is a big mistake.

Sure, Bratton vies with Rudy for public attention. The police commissioner's job is the most glamorous in government and someone like Bratton who has charismatic qualities will receive an even greater share of attention than might otherwise be the case.

Bratton also had a superb spokesperson in John Miller, who deserves commendation for achieving high recognition for the NYPD in the public's consciousness. When Miller resigned last week, he did go too far in his comments when he said, "I'm loyal to the mayor. I'm loyal to the police commissioner. But there were loyal Nazis, too." Rudy should know New Yorkers will tolerate a Boston accent in their police commissioner, but never in their mayor.

The mayor's policy of forcing commissioners to put people on their staffs—as opposed to simply asking that they consider certain individuals—has damaged both the agencies and Rudy's relationships with commissioners.

I am told that commissioners are now so afraid of the mayor and his inner circle of advisors that the former carefully close their office doors when the conversation turns to City Hall. Fear—not respect—walks the corridors of the agencies.

That bodes ill for the mayor, who is entering a period of serious retrenchment in the delivery of services and will need commissioners, deputies, and those in middle-level government positions to do their best to preserve the present while looking to the future. Instead, they are busy looking over their shoulders wondering how long, how long...

I believe in a strong mayoral presence, and one that leads by example. But leadership based on fear breeds resentment and mounting anger. An army that feels threatened by its own general is less likely to win a war, even if such a general wins early skirmishes—as Rudy has, to his great credit.

It is not too late to change course. But time is running out. When the devastating cuts required to balance the budget kick in—for which Rudy should not be blamed, but will be by many who will suffer—the mayor will need that army to be supportive. If treated with suspicion and contempt, they will turn on him at the first opportunity. Rudy has reached the hubris stage in 14 months. It took me 12 years.

NEW YORK POST   JUNE 23, 1995

THE MAYOR AND THE CHANCELLOR

Giuliani's latest crisis is entirely self-inflicted

Under Rudy Giuliani, New York city has gone through several fiscal crises, as it did under both David Dinkins and me. The city's financial strength in the private sector is so strong that it weathered every such past crisis—and it will weather the current one as well.

However, the mayor is now dealing with a different crisis—one that is self-generated. I believe it was his unceasing personal attacks that caused Schools Chancellor Ramon Cortines to resign.

The mayor engaged in unacceptable language when he described Cortines as "whining," "precious," and playing the "little victim" and announced that he should "grow up."

Cortines undoubtedly thought to himself: "I'm being dumped on by the mayor every single day. He didn't even call to congratulate me when the reading and math scores went up. I'm going to leave now at a high, and lets see how he does without me."

Every recent mayor—including the incumbent—has complained that the present state of the law makes it difficult, even impossible, for the city's school system to function as well as it could. The mayor is held responsible for the state of public education— translated as the ability of students to read, write, use math, and speak standard English— but he lacks the ability to substantially and substantively have impact on it via the Board of Education.

Legally, the board is totally independent of the mayor—notwithstanding the fact that they receive 25 percent of the City's annual budget.

During Mayor Wagner's administration, every member of the Board of Education was appointed by the mayor. But in 1969, the state legislature, seeking to punish John Lindsay for proposing and implementing decentralization—which was followed by chaos and racial and ethnic battles—stripped the mayor of the right to make any appointments to the board and gave that authority to the five borough presidents.

Four years later, the board was expanded from five to seven members and the mayor was given two appointments; the others still belonged to the borough presidents.

This, regrettably, prevented the possibility of the mayor creating a philosophical majority on the board. Such a majority, if effective, would lay out a blueprint for a chancellor selected by the board members to implement their plan in keeping with that common philosophy.

The board itself, most experts on education believe, should not seek to make day-to-day decisions or engage in policy implementation—that's the job of the chancellor.

Even though he lacks a majority on the board, mayor Giuliani has decided to play an aggressive—indeed hostile—role vis-à-vis that board. He also announced that he expects to have a major—and, from his language, perhaps dominant—role in the selection of a new chancellor.

On his weekly radio show last Friday, Giuliani said: "What we're going to try to do is, right from the very beginning, try to impress on the board the fact that it's counter-productive to select a chancellor that isn't selected with significant input and approval by the mayor and by city government, by City Hall."

When I criticize the mayor, some say, "But you yourself tried to get control of the Board of Education." That's not correct. I sought to get the state legislature to put into law the state Board of Regents' long-standing proposal to expand the board, with the mayor appointing 10 of 15 members instead of the current structure.

The Regents' proposal, if implemented, would not give the mayor control of the board. Once the mayor made the appointments, giving the board a core-majority philosophy, the members—hopefully first-rate educators—would be independent of the mayor and have a fixed four-year term, not removable except for cause.

However, that was never achieved and is not the current law. And if you're the mayor, you must never forget you're not above the law: Hubris is a mayor's greatest enemy.

Mayor Giuliani now must bear the responsibility of the disruption and turmoil that will in all probability ensue as a result of Chancellor Cortines' resignation. If history teaches us anything, he'll find that the search for a new chancellor inevitably opens up a Pandora's box of rivalry between the different racial and ethnic groups in this town.

I hope it doesn't happen—but it's happened before.

Cortines was driven out, but he went out with great grace. There's only one way to persuade him to stay, but it's wishful thinking on my part. Rudy could apologize and say "I made a mistake"—just like Fiorello LaGuardia, who said, "When I make a mistake, it's a beaut."

Unfortunately, I don't think he's capable of doing that. Besides, at this point Cortines probably wouldn't change his mind—even if Rudy could bring himself to apologize.

I believe in a strong mayoral presence. But leadership based on fear breeds resentment. Everyone knows that I always had an open door at City Hall and that every member of my staff felt free to tell me exactly what he or she thought, without fear of the consequences. The only limitation for them was that once I'd decided on a policy, they could continue to argue with me and try to change my mind—but they could not attack the policy in public.

Mayor Giuliani is first-rate when it comes to substance. But he has to learn to respect others who disagree with him. His interpersonal relationships rival those of Frankenstein's monster.

I predict the next resignation will be that of Police Commissioner Bill Bratton, who has performed superbly. Rudy demeaned him by requiring that Bratton fire his very able press secretary, John Miller, because Rudy apparently resented the accolades and positive press that Bratton was receiving.

When I was mayor, I wanted the police commissioner to get all the attention and applause possible—and then I would bask in his reflected glory, saying "I appointed him."

Pride goeth before a fall. Doesn't it make sense to avoid that fall?

Rudy responds to the business community, as he should. After all, they create the industry, jobs, and revenues that make it possible to pay for and deliver services. And the two paramount services provided by government are education and safety.

Mayor Giuliani—like Mayor Dinkins before him—has done a superb job in enhancing the efficiency of the police department and increasing its ranks. Regrettably, education has not been similarly attended.

The civic leaders in this city—and there are dozens of them—should be knocking on the mayor's door, urging a more balanced approach by both the mayor and the Board of Education. Their working together is essential if our children are to excel.

'CONTROL FREAK' RUDY RISKS DEFEAT AT POLLS

It's not enough for a mayor to be an effective administrator

Rudy Giuliani is no Fiorello LaGuardia. When LaGuardia erred, he was capable of saying "When I make a mistake, it's a beaut." Rudy cannot admit error.

There is blame on both sides when it comes to the chancellor debacle. But the mayor's failures are greater than those of the Board of Education.

Under the law, the Board is a independent entity. Like other mayors before him, Rudy wants to change that. I thought the Board should be expanded to 15 members with five members appointed by the borough presidents and the remaining ten appointed by the mayor. Regrettably, I couldn't get to first base with the State Legislature.

Rudy may have better luck with his proposal to eliminate the Board and Chancellor entirely and appoint a commissioner reporting to him with City Council oversight. He may even establish that total mayoral control is the better way to go, although I don't think so.

But as things now stand, he has violated the spirit of the law by saying to the Board, in effect, "The law may say you are independent, but I am now going to turn you into a mayoral agency."

Post columnist Jack Newfield, a friend and political supporter of Rudy's, recently wrote, "Two years ago,

Rudy Giuliani promised us a reformist, anti-patronage, anti-machine government...By supporting [Leon] Goldstein [for Chancellor], Mayor Giuliani is breaking faith with his reformist, anti-clubhouse covenant..."

I agree with Newfield's ultimate assessment: "The only explanation for Giuliani embracing Goldstein is the mayor's mania for control."

By blocking the Board's selection of Daniel Domenech, after Goldstein had the good sense to withdraw, the mayor won the current Board of Ed battle. But one wonders what the mayor said to Jerry Camarata, the Staten Island appointee to the Board, to get him to change his initial yes vote to a no 24 hours later.

I think state Senator Roy Goodman (R-Man.), chairman of the Committee on Investigations, Taxation and Government Operations, should hold public hearings and take testimony to learn exactly what was said.

Instead of trying to run the Board of Ed, the mayor should turn his attention to an agency over which he does have total authority under the law – the Human Resources Administration.

Last weekend, state Supreme Court Justice Helen Freedman announced, after touring the Emergency Assistance Unit that serves as the citywide intake center, that she may appoint an independent director to oversee the city's system for sheltering homeless families. During the tour, the *New York Times* reported, she found "people with serious medical problems, an abundance of flies buzzing around the office and women and families with weeks-old babies spending the night in the over-crowded center."

Justice Freedman was quoted as saying, "What was most distressing was the sickness and the amount of time people were there, basically living on plastic chairs and floors all crowded together."

This is the same judge who charged the City with contempt during the Dinkins administration for failing to adequately shelter homeless families. She even threatened to have David Dinkins' first deputy mayor, Norman Steisel, and his Human Resources Administration commissioner, Barbara "I don't talk to the press" Sabol, spend a night in a shelter.

The Giuliani administration has not implemented a plan to correct the deficiencies of his predecessor. How many times, if ever, has Rudy personally visited the EAU after midnight to see the conditions for himself?

Before he criticizes the Board of Ed, he needs to provide adequate physical and medical care for those same children now in his direct charge whose education he would like to control.

In any situation involving the mayor and an independent agency like the Board of Ed, there will always be some pushing and shoving, as there is with the MTA and the Port Authority. But the mayor must also show respect for the agency while criticizing it.

The Board of Ed is not without fault. It has displayed poor judgment, but to a lesser degree than has Rudy, who is seeking to usurp—without authority—the authority of the Board.

When Leon Goldstein withdrew and they were down to two candidates, the Board of Ed should have opened the search again. But that's a judgment call. Perhaps they concluded they had culled the best and it made no sense to further delay the appointment process.

As for Goldstein, it was foolhardy for Rudy to endorse him, especially once he knew of Goldstein's failure to be candid. One reporter told me experience shows that when someone in public life engages in a string of false statements on small maters, they will ultimately fail the test of probity on larger matters because it's become a way of life.

Rudy Giuliani conveyed his total disrespect for the chancellor and the Board of Ed by his language and actions. He drove Ray Cortines out of town. His rhetoric was unacceptable, using language which should not be used to describe anyone, let alone a person with the talent, intelligence, and integrity that Cortines has displayed since he arrived.

When Rudy described Cortines as "whining," "precious" and playing the "little victim," what was he seeking to convey other than to totally demean him—or worse? When he held meetings with candidates for chancellor, he vilely insulted Board of Ed president Carol Gresser, saying the discussions were "beyond Carol Gresser's ability to carry on a substantive discussion."

For a mayor to be a great mayor, there are two requirements: One, that he/she be a superb administrator. Rudy is—in contrast with David Dinkins.

But it is not enough to be an administrator, no matter how good. It is essential that the mayor of the City of New York display an understanding of the needs, anxieties, expectations, and hopes that people have. New York's mayor is traditionally a father figure.

In this regard, David Dinkins shone: people believed he was concerned about them. In contrast, when speaking of Rudy, many people describe him as ruthless, uncaring and prosecutorial.

At the present time, Rudy and his supporters—of which I continue to be one, his gross lapses in judgment notwithstanding—believe that if the election were held tomorrow, Rudy would win hands down. But not because people will vote for Rudy, so much as vote against a return to the left-wing politics of his likely opponents.

If Rudy continues down this path of constant confrontation, seeking to wipe the mat with his opponents, he may not be reelected. And that would be a pity.

NEW YORK POST   JANUARY 5, 1996

WHY RUDY'S WRONG ON JUDGES

His selection approach would have a chilling effect on their integrity and independence

Judges Eugene Schwartzwald and Jerome Kay may or may not be qualified to be reappointed to the Criminal Court. But that was a decision to be made by the two judicial screening panels, the Mayor's Advisory Committee on the Judiciary and the City Bar Association—not Rudy Giuliani.

Yet instead of adhering to this independent, non-political process, Mayor Giuliani overruled the panels after they had recommended that the two judges be reappointed.

In doing that, as a *New York Times* editorial put it, "The argument shifted from a debate about the quality of judges to the fitness of Mr. Giuliani as judicial arbiter."

When I came into office in 1978, I created the Mayor's Advisory Committee on the Judiciary so that all potential candidates for judgeships would go through its members. The panel then chose three candidates for each open office. I met with those candidates and chose one. On occasion, I would reject all three and ask the committee to send me three more.

As the *Times* pointed out, merit selection "was one of Mr. Koch's great achievements, and Mayor Giuliani's refusal to acknowledge that during this spitting match is a stark example of his worst failure as a leader—the compulsion to denounce everyone who disagrees with him."

Yet Giuliani foolishly and falsely said at a press conference, as reported in the *Post*: "You can search our record over and over again, inside and out... and you can't find even the suggestion of a political appointment to the bench. Neither Mayor Dinkins nor Mayor Koch can say that with any credibility."

In being criticized by the mayor, I was in the good company of Chief Judge Judith Kaye, who met with the mayor early last month to encourage him to reappoint the two judges. For this, Giuliani, according to the *Times*, "criticized her for criticizing him, saying she had overstepped her bounds."

Why all the sturm und drang? Because judges should make their rulings without worrying that they must please the mayor. They should only have to convince peers on a screening panel that they are worthy of reappointment. Otherwise, their independence is chilled and their integrity impaired.

Our current Caesar threatens to expand this pernicious practice. According to the *Times*, "Mr. Giuliani, furious, said that if anything he planned to remove more sitting judges from the bench when their terms ended, calling it his job to clean up the legacy of shady, politically motivated judicial appointments perpetuated by Mr. Dinkins and Mr. Koch."

The greatest outrage on Giuliani's part was reported by *Newsday*: "Giuliani, speaking at City Hall, blasted his two predecessors saying their 200-plus appointments to the bench were dominated by the influence of former political bosses Donald Manes, Stanley Friedman and Meade Esposito."

That is an outright lie. As the *Times* editorial notes, "Mr. Giuliani and his aides suggested, with no evidence whatsoever, that Mayors Koch and Dinkins had practiced behind-the-scenes politics to influence the process and reward loyal Democrats with judgeships."

Giuliani is simply engaging in what he does best—character assassination and brutalizing his critics. He's even been known to demean individuals in his own administration.

There are other examples: His personal attacks on former schools Chancellor Ramon Cortines, describing him as "whining," "precious," and playing the "little victim"; his eliminating Board of Education President Carol Gresser from meetings with chancellor candidates, saying the discussions were "beyond Carol Gresser's ability to carry on a substantive discussion," and his forcing out Police Commissioner William Bratton's press secretary, John Miller, referring to the press operation as "out of control" and "dangerous"—all because he believed the police commissioner was receiving too much credit for reducing crime.

Now we see his public attacks on Judge Schwartzwald, embarrassing the judge and his family by saying he lacks "the intellectual capacity to try cases," and his assault on Chief Judge Kaye for daring to question his decision not to reappoint the two sitting judges.

When David Dinkins and I jointly denounced Rudy's tampering with the merit-selection process that I created to eliminate political involvement by outsiders and the mayor, Rudy did what he always does when criticized—lunge for the jugular and engage in every conceivable slander.

The mayor even employed Joseph McCarthy tactics by waving around a book written by two reporters who were hostile to me, twice repeating a partial line from it about "the Koch collapse on judicial selection." *Times* columnist Joyce Purnick reached for the book and pointed out that the mayor failed to note "that the reference was to a different process and court—a 1979 nomination for the State Supreme Court, an elective position unrelated to the Koch judicial screening committee, and his own judicial appointments."

Joseph Welch's statement during the Army-McCarthy hearings seems particularly apropos: "Have you no sense of decency, sir?"

The mayor claims he took this action because he wants judges to be of the "very highest quality." Ironically, in condemning Judge Schwartzwald the mayor cited the fact that in 1977, under then-mayor Abe Beame, Schwartzwald was rejected by two judicial screening committees; Giuliani then alleged that Schwartzwald was unable to try cases.

It now develops, according to the *Post*, that one of Rudy's appointees, Charles A. Posner, as a top aide to Brooklyn DA Joe Hynes, "only tried seven cases in six years, and in each case he was the 'second seat,' assisting a more experienced prosecutor."

Rudy's other appointee, Robert E. Torres, according to the *Times*, "flunked out of Brooklyn Law School twice and never earned a law degree but became a lawyer by studying on his own and passing the bar exam." The *Times* went on to say that Torres had applied for a seat on the bench before three other committees—mine, David Dinkins' and Mario Cuomo's—none of which approved him.

With all due deference to Judge Torres, Giuliani's comparing him to Abraham Lincoln is a bit of a stretch.

If Rudy wants to raise judicial standards, all he has to do is direct the committee to raise theirs. But by substituting his judgment for theirs, as Gary Brown, executive director of the Fund for Modern Courts said, "This may very well have a chilling effect on judges."

Unfortunately, Rudy is what he is and cannot change. Heraclitus said, "A man's character is his fate."

A TALE OF TWO JUDGES

Two judges, three decisions, two conclusions. One, Harold Baer Jr., is a federal judge with life tenure. The other, David Friedman, is a Criminal Court judge with a renewable term of ten years.

In the federal-court case, Carol Bayless was arrested last year after, according to the Post, "plain-clothes cops spotted her driving a 1995 Caprice slowly at 176th Street and Amsterdam Avenue about 5 a.m. The cops told [Judge] Baer they became suspicious when four men loaded two duffel bags into Bayless' car trunk without speaking to her, then ran off when they spotted the officers." This occurred in Washington Heights, the drug center of New York City, and the car had an out-of-state license plate.

Judge Baer threw out the evidence—34 kilograms of cocaine and two kilos of heroin found in the car—as well as Bayless' taped confession, in which she admitted driving from Detroit to New York with $1 million in cash in the trunk to pick up drugs; she had done so more that 20 times since 1991.

Judge Baer chose to disbelieve the police officers' sworn testimony that the men ran. He did so on the basis of the defendant's videotaped statement wherein she said that the men had not run. Her statement was in direct conflict with those of the police officers and, of course, she was not subject to cross-examination.

Judge Baer demonstrated his anti-police bias when he added, "Residents in this neighborhood [Washington

Heights] tended to regard police officers as corrupt, abusive, and violent. Had the men not run when the cops began to stare at them, it would have been unusual... What I find shattering is that, in this day and age, blacks in black neighborhoods and blacks in white neighborhoods can count on little security for their person."

In the state Criminal Court case, Judge David Friedman ruled evidence collected in a Brooklyn rape case was not admissible because police had conducted the search after 9 P.M. The Consolidated Laws of New York, Sec. 690.30 (2) provides: "A search warrant may be executed only between the hours of 6 A.M. and 9 P.M., unless the warrant expressly authorizes execution thereof at any time of the day or night."

In both cases, the judges were excoriated by large numbers of public officials.

Judge Baer's decision flies in the face of common sense. In order for a judge to sustain the stop-and-search action of the cops, he had to find that the cops had "reasonable suspicion" to stop the driver and search the car trunk. Judge Baer's tortured treatment of the facts and circumstances in concluding that there was no "reasonable suspicion"; his out-of-hand rejection of the police officers' testimony with respect to flight—always evidence of guilt—based upon a statement of a defendant never subjected to cross-examination; and his statement that the men were correct to run when they saw the police, evidences an anti-law-enforcement bias which is appalling.

In a final stroke, he branded the U.S. Attorney's efforts to have him reconsider the case "a juvenile project."

On the other hand, the case before Judge Friedman was open and shut—with no discretion. The law is clear—but not to the *Daily News* editorial board, which demagogically denounced Friedman, stating: "The cops' 'intrusion' supposedly violated the defendant's privacy. Would that the judge was equally concerned with the 'intrusion' upon the rape victim."

Judges must uphold laws with which we may disagree. Warrants executed late at night—as they were in Nazi and Communist-dominated countries to heighten citizens' fear of the government—may generate greater resistance, even in a democracy.

In the case of Judge Friedman, it now develops that the Brooklyn District Attorney's office was delinquent in not refuting the defense counsel's allegation that the search warrant was executed after 9 p.m. The matter has now become moot. Earlier this week, pointing out the defense counsel's error, Judge Friedman reversed his decision and ruled that the seized evidence could be admitted.

Judge Friedman deserves applause for both decisions. He did what the law required and then what the new evidence warranted. One hopes that Judge Baer, on the motion filed by the U.S. Attorney Tuesday, will do the same.

Concerning the reappointment of judges, Mayor Giuliani has announced it will be his standard of excellence that applies, not those of the two appointing committees: the Association of the Bar and the Mayor's Advisory Committee on the Judiciary.

Irrespective of their entire record of excellence, the reappointment of judges who have made controversial decisions similar to those of Judge Baer or Judge Friedman could be in jeopardy.

As a federal judge, Judge Baer has life tenure. But if he did not, and I were still mayor, I would reappoint both him and Judge Friedman—if the two screening committees recommended reappointment. Reappointment should be based on a judge's entire record, as recommended by the two committees.

The Association of the Bar—supporting my criticism of Mayor Giuliani for politicizing the appointment of judges—has said through its president, Barbara Paul Robinson:

"While the standards should be sufficiently high to approve only well qualified incumbents, once met, incumbent judges should be reappointed. Otherwise, there is a real danger that, at the very least, there will be an appearance of politics intruding into the decisions of the courts. A judge who has been approved by both Judiciary Committees should not have to worry whether a particular Mayor will find them appropriate for re-appointment."

It is interesting how so many lawyers have chosen to remain silent, undoubtedly out of fear of the mayor's vindictiveness. One lawyer recently said to me, "I'm so glad you stood up to the mayor and spoke out."

I replied, "It would be even better if you did."

Another told me on the phone, "You are right and I'd like to speak out, but I am part of an organization that gets funds from the city and I'm afraid he'd cut them off."

God save us from those wielding absolute power. If we cannot go back to the total merit-selection system, then the State Legislature should give the City Council the power to "advise and consent" for future appointments to the Criminal and Family Courts—as the State Senate has with respect to gubernatorial judicial appointments to the Court of Claims and Court of Appeals and the U.S. Senate has for the presidential appointment of federal judges.

SOME HITS, MORE MISSES

Last week, *Post* Op-Ed columnist Hilton Kramer accused me of embarking on a "senseless public vendetta" against Mayor Giuliani. Ironic, given that Kramer's weekly column is an unending diatribe against the *New York Times*.

I've decided to address the issue by pointing out how I've both praised and criticized the mayor.

So, first, in praise of Rudy Giuliani...

He and Police Commissioner Bill Bratton deserve the thanks of New Yorkers for a city where crimes of violence have been reduced to an even greater extent than in the nation as a whole. The mayor deserves great credit for taking on organized crime at the Fulton Fish Market.

Courageously, he did not curry the Policeman's Benevolent Association (PBA) favor, and instead fought the PBA's ultimately successful effort to push through legislation in Albany that authorizes it to do an end run around New York City's collective-bargaining process.

Bravely, he eliminated affirmative action programs based on race, ethnicity and gender that David Dinkins had created by executive order. He successfully took on the striking Legal Aid lawyers, as well as the illegal peddlers on 125th Street.

Those are the highlights. Now, to the criticisms—which require more background.

The mayor's latest financial plan is full of holes. According to the *Times*, "A major credit rating agency, Moody's Investors Service, said the City's bond rating, already among the lowest of any major city, could fall further." Richard P. Larkin, managing director of Standard & Poor's, said, "It's pretty much what we expected when we lowered the rating (last year). The city continues to live year to year."

Seeking to divert the fiscal monitors, the press, and the public, the mayor spoke of his concern for children, saying a budget "must be compassionate" and "must balance the needs of people."

However, within ten days after publishing the financial plan, the mayor announced $700 million in additional cuts. It is inconceivable that he was unaware of the need for these cuts when he announced his fiscal plan—he was governing by delayed press release.

Earlier, the mayor agreed to a three-year, no-layoff provision for all municipal workers, except those at the Health and Hospitals Corporation: A political act, costly to the city, to obtain union support in his re-election campaign.

For me, Mayor Giuliani's single greatest error was ending the merit-selection system in the reappointment of judges, which I created. Barbara Paul Robinson, president of the prestigious Association of the Bar, criticized his actions, saying, "A judge who has been approved by both Judiciary committees should not have to worry whether a particular mayor will find them appropriate for reappointment."

After David Dinkins and I criticized him, the mayor falsely stated, "None of this is addressed by former Mayor Dinkins or former Mayor Koch, both of whom perpetuated on the bench a significant number of Democratic machine politicians despite their hypocritical allegiance to some pristine process. I happen to know that process because I investigated that process."

What was the outcome of that investigation, conducted by Rudy Giuliani presumably when he was U.S.

Attorney? Who got indicted? Is it fair to smear me and all the members of the two committees connected with the process without revealing any factual basis for it?

Having politicized the re-appointment of judges, the mayor has now moved on to the Police Department, telling Commissioner Bratton whom to promote among high-ranking commanders, instead of letting him exercise his own professional judgment. The mayor sought to defend his conduct by citing his law enforcement expertise. But he was a prosecutor, not a police officer.

Illustrating the Giuliani administration's politicizing of the NYPD, the Times reported: "An adviser to Mr. Bratton said aides to the Mayor had raised questions about the loyalty of Chief [Jules] Martin, who served as the commanding officer of the police intelligence unit that provided security for City Hall and Gracie Mansion during the Dinkins administration. 'They wanted to know if he had made any public statements in favor of the Mayor,' said the adviser. 'They said he was a Dinkins man and we don't think he's loyal.'"

In my administration, the only police appointment I ever made was that of commissioner—who then made all other appointments without consulting me. That's the way it should be in the NYPD.

The mayor's willingness to bear false witness, his meanspiritedness, and his bully tactics are major character flaws. And character is fate. This conclusion led me to tell a recent gathering that Mayor Giuliani "is a good administrator, but he's not a decent human being."

I referred to his unacceptable personal attacks on others. The mayor described former Schools Chancellor Ramon Cortines, whom he drove out of town, as "precious," "whining," and playing the "little victim." He insulted Board of Education President Carol Carol

Gresser in the most sexist language, saying the issues were "beyond Carol Gresser to carry on a substantive discussion."

I have also joined City Comptroller Alan Hevesi in criticizing Giuliani for seeking to sell the city's water resources to the Water Board in order to use those revenues to pay for school repairs—a worthy project that should be otherwise funded. The comptroller pointed out that the Water Board was created only to expand and repair the water system itself—not to fund other city needs.

Hevesi won the lawsuit filed against him by the mayor and the City Council, saving consumers from the rate increases that would have been necessary to service the debt on the billions in bonds the board would have issued to make the purchase. Nevertheless, Mayor Giuliani claimed victory—so why is he appealing?

In a true human tragedy, Elisa Izquierdo, a child allegedly murdered by her mother, was left unprotected by the Human Resources Administration and Child Welfare Agency, which failed in their responsibility for her safety. Instead of demanding resignations, Mayor Giuliani praised CWA and its commissioner.

After editorial writers and others denounced the agency, the mayor finally appointed a new commissioner and detached it from HRA. But he allowed the former commissioner to remain on as first deputy.

In 1993, when asked about my endorsement of Rudy Giuliani, I responded, "Ah, to be 68 and still relevant." In 1997, at age 72, I hope to still be relevant and do that which is then in the best interest of the city. But would I like to be 35 again? You bet.

NEW YORK POST   **APRIL, 6 1996**

GREEK TRAGEDY AT CITY HALL

Approximately two years into Mayor Giuliani's first term, we see a bruised and battered mayor. He has had a number of significant substantive successes—but also several major failures resulting from character flaws.

My support of Rudy Giuliani in 1993 was based on my conclusion that the city needed a change in leadership. Giuliani and I were not personal friends, although we had worked together when I was mayor and he was U.S. Attorney.

When the corruption scandal at the Parking Violations Bureau was revealed, I appreciated the fact that Giuliani said, "I think I know as much about these investigations as anyone knows, including a lot of confidential material, and there's not a single shred of evidence or suggestion that Mayor Koch knew of crimes that were being committed by several of the Democratic leaders and the borough presidents, or had any involvement in those crimes, or would have done anything other than turn them in if he had found out about them."

I called Giuliani at the time to thank him. He said he had only done that which was right. After his unsuccessful prosecution of Judge Hortense Gabel and Bess Myerson, the press asked me whether he had been overzealous in pursuing the case. I said he had to bring the case based on the evidence before him. Giuliani told me he was very appreciative of my comments because morale at his office was very low due to the criticisms.

My serious doubts concerning Mayor Giuliani's personality and character, unspoken at the time, actually began in a telephone call by the mayor to me in late 1994. He called to tell me why the police had torn down gubernatorial campaign posters—a move I had criticized. He began by saying there was a law against putting such posters on city property. When I sought to comment, he brusquely interjected, "Don't interrupt me."

I was shocked and, as I subsequently reported, cradled the phone in my shoulder and started to read my mail. Had he allowed me to speak, I would have said I knew it was illegal, since the law was passed during my administration. But that's a law you enforce the day after the election—and why were only Pataki's posters torn down? (Giuliani had endorsed Cuomo.)

I believe we are seeing a Greek tragedy unfold. The mayor's tragic flaws, hubris, and a compulsion to blame others for his errors and those of his administration, are bubbling to the surface, with increasingly harmful consequences for the city.

Consider the evidence: We all witnessed the mayor's efforts to demean Schools Chancellor Ramon Cortines. Mayor Giuliani did not merely attack the chancellor's positions, he launched vicious, personal attacks.

New York City was blessed with an excellent police commissioner, Bill Bratton. The police and the public respected him and appreciated his successes. The mayor, unable to tolerate the competition, drove him out.

We again witnessed the mayor's need to demean when highly respected UN official Gillian Sorensen sought to advise the mayor not to eject Yasser Arafat from Lincoln Center, reportedly saying, "Mr. Mayor, you cannot do that. Chairman Arafat is part of the UN commemoration and is here as an official observer. He is here at the approval of the U.S. and has tickets for the concert."

The mayor rudely rebuffed her wise counsel, saying, "Gillian, I don't want to hear it."

Not until the mayor partially destroyed the merit judicial-selection system did I state I could not conceive endorsing him again. When David Dinkins and I criticized his action, instead of simply defending his position Giuliani attacked our integrity—falsely stating: "None of this is addressed by former Mayor Dinkins or former Mayor Koch, both of whom perpetuated on the bench a significant number of Democratic machine politicians despite their hypocritical allegiance to some pristine process. I happen to know that process because I investigated that process."

Regrettably, that is Mayor Giuliani's stock in trade. When under attack, he will falsely charge his critics with improprieties.

About nine months ago, I warned the mayor that Commissioner Bratton would leave if he continued to demean him. He responded, "I don't care if he leaves. I run the Police Department."

When I alluded to his comment publicly months later, Giuliani at a press conference denied having said it—another indication of his willingness to dissemble. In view of what he has since done to Bratton, does anyone now doubt he made that statement?

Yet it was still shocking to learn, according to the *Times*, that Giuliani tried to "micro-manage the (police) department, overruling transfers of senior commanders and even precinct detectives."

More generally, every administration—and the Giuliani administration is no exception—has within it occasional corruption. The mayor is always politically responsible, even if he is not personally involved or has no prior knowledge of it. The question should be: How did the mayor react when informed?

When City comptroller Alan Hevesi brought to public attention what he described as the "bizarre" awarding of a $43 million city contract to HANAC (Hellenic American Neighborhood Action Committee)— a Queens organization which was neither lowest bidder (HANAC's bid was $8 million higher) or highest performer—Giuliani denounced Hevesi, defended his agency, and said the contract process had been marked by brave and heroic decisions.

U.S. Attorney Mary Jo White has issued subpoenas and the Giuliani administration has belatedly canceled the contract, following further disclosures that HANAC hired the brother of a top mayoral aide. True to itself, the administration accepts no responsibility – even though the First Deputy Mayor personally approved the contract.

If he were still U.S. attorney, the mayor undoubtedly would have denounced his contract agency immediately; instead he attacked the low bidder, which, according to Hevesi should have been awarded the contract. As *Times* columnist Joyce Purnick wrote, "Every time something goes wrong, the mayor finds a scapegoat."

As Hevesi, a possible challenger in next year's election put it, "Wouldn't it be wonderful if someday the mayor recognized that it's not always someone else's fault?"

Next to the mayor, the police commissioner and schools chancellor are the City's two most important public servants. The mayor has now deprived the city of top-notch individuals in those roles: Ramon Cortines and Bill Bratton. And he has caused the NYPD to undergo enormous turmoil.

Rudy has a year and a half to recoup—but as Caesar said, "The fault, dear Brutus, is not in our stars; but in ourselves."

Brutus asked, "Upon what meat doth this our Caesar feed?"

I hope it's not British beef.

WHEN POLITICIANS TRY TO INTIMIDATE JUDGES

"No man's life, liberty or property are safe while the legislature is in session," said a Surrogate of the State of New York in 1866.

There are occasions when something similar can be said about chief executives ranging from mayors and governors to presidents. In our constitutional system, we rely on an independent judiciary to protect us from authoritarian executives and capricious actions of legislatures.

All winter, controversy has raged concerning the independence of the judiciary. With the spring thaw, the storm has not abated. Federal Judge Harold Baer's decision to suppress evidence in a drug case was roundly criticized by President Clinton, Senate Majority Leader Bob Dole, and House Speaker Newt Gingrich—not to mention Governor Pataki, Mayor Giuliani, every editorial board in town, and myself.

As a federal judge, Harold Baer has the constitutional protection of a lifetime appointment, removable only for high crimes and misdemeanors. But after Dole and Gingrich urged his impeachment, and the White House press secretary announced that President Clinton might ask the judge to resign unless he changed his decision, Baer capitulated and reversed himself. In doing so, he further destroyed his independence.

More recently, Criminal Court Judge Loren Duckman was criticized for two egregious rulings concerning bail and sentencing in domestic violence cases. Following the rulings, both Pataki and Giuliani demanded that Duckman be investigated by the Commission on Judicial Conduct and impeached by the State Senate—and both asked that the judge voluntarily retire from the bench forthwith. Their criticisms have grown into intimidation and harassment. Last week the Commission on Judicial Conduct said "there is no evidence that Judge Duckman engaged in judicial misconduct in the exercise of [this] discretionary authority" in either case.

The Commission did recommend formal charges against the judge for two other matters concerning alleged improper treatment of prosecutors and charges of racism. In one instance, Judge Duckman allegedly referred to a female assistant district attorney as "sexy" and in another he called a confrontation between two black women "cultural."

The governor and the mayor, outraged by its rejection of the original charges, denounced the commission; both men also again urged Duckman to resign. Giuliani also encouraged the governor to recommend impeachment proceedings to the State Senate, a move Pataki has said he would consider if the commission did not reconsider the original charges against the judge.

Giuliani's latest comments on junk justice relate to his own appointee, Judge Donna Recant, who set $1,000 bail for one defendant and no bail for the other in a statutory rape case.

While suggesting he "might have increased the bail asked for by the prosecutor" to $15,000 or $20,000, Giuliani added that "the judge made a reasonable decision... This is an area in which reasonable minds can differ about the application of the law to the facts."

One can certainly question whether Judge Recant acted appropriately—but I question whether Mayor

Giuliani would have been so kind had he not appointed her less than a year ago. Judge Duckman's problem is that he was appointed by David Dinkins. I guess it depends on whose judge is being gored.

With respect to the larger issue, if the current federal and state laws are inadequate with respect to appeals from judicial decisions, then change the law, not the judges.

To many, including me, the actions of both Judge Baer and Judge Duckman were clearly foolish. But we as a society would be even more foolish to encourage and support those who are oblivious to the need for an independent judiciary. Therein lies the danger.

Unlike the federal and state court judges, where judicial appointees (as opposed to those who are elected) are subject to ratification by the U.S. or state Senate, the 140 mayoral appointments require no ratification.

When I came into office, I made a commitment on judicial reappointments: If both the Mayor's Advisory committee on the Judiciary and the City Bar Association recommended that a sitting judge be reappointed, I would reappoint that person—without exception. And, if either of those two screening committees recommended that a sitting judge not be reappointed, I would, again without exception, follow this advice.

Regrettably, on July 20, 1994, Mayor Giuliani issued an executive order with new language giving him the right unilaterally to reject a reappointment—even when both committees recommended reappointment of a judge whose term was expiring.

Last December, the mayor did not reappoint two Criminal Court judges despite the fact that both had been recommended for the second time for reappointment by his committees. Giuliani's actions were criticized by former Mayor Dinkins and myself, along with Judith Kaye, presiding Justice of the New York Court of Appeals; Barbara Paul Robinson, president of the City Bar Association; Francis Murphy, presiding Justice of the Appellate Division, First Department; and editorial boards of the *New York Times* and *Crain's New York Business*.

In dictatorships and juntas—and they exist throughout the world—judges do the bidding of the government as expressed by the executive. In democratic countries, we normally defend the independence of the judiciary. Apparently, this isn't true at this time in our history.

When judges in a democratic society have to fear being demeaned, publicly denounced, and threatened with removal, the concept of an independent judiciary becomes meaningless. Many judges will soon become compliant and succumb to the pressures of a chief executive who threatens not to reappoint—or, worse still, to seek impeachment not for high crimes and misdemeanors, but because he or she disagrees with particular rulings.

The City of New York is the largest litigant in the City's civil and criminal courts. Must the average citizen bringing an action worry about the outcome now that judges have to think about the mayor's desired result, or else be threatened that they won't be reappointed?

Doesn't it send a chill when the governor can call for and initiate impeachment? Or that other high-profile officials, like the President, Senate Majority Leader, and Speaker of the House, have the power to demean and destroy a judge's reputation?

How does a federal judge respond if the President calls and says, "I appointed you. You have embarrassed me. I ask you in good conscience to step down."?

Not every recipient of such a call will have the temerity to just say no.

MY GIULIANI PROBLEM
I supported him in '93—but next year is a different matter

Last weekend, on Channel 2 News, Mayor Giuliani was asked to assess his Democratic competition in next year's election. Understandably, he described all of the possible candidates as overwhelmingly flawed.

Less understandably, the mayor made clear his intent to run against the record of former Mayor David Dinkins, no matter who he ends up facing. Willie Horton deja vu.

I helped the mayor win the last time around, but I won't be supporting him this time. Why? Because Rudy Giuliani has failed as our mayor.

Yes, he's had enormous successes in reducing crime (even taking into account the published Police Department Admission that crime statistics were altered in several of the City's 76 police precincts). Giuliani deserves credit for taking on organized crime in the Fulton Fish Market, Hunts Point Market, and the San Gennaro Festival.

But a mayor must be more than a cop. Regrettably, that's all Rudy is. The next mayor might consider offering him the position of police commissioner, since Giuliani has made clear that he already runs the NYPD.

Rudy will probably receive the editorial endorsements of the four major city newspapers. If an election were held next Tuesday, he would win. He may win next year, too—but I believe he will lose. Am I sorry that I supported him in 1993? No, given the choice and the Crown Heights unchecked pogrom.

Substantively, Giuliani's greatest blunders to date are politicizing the merit judicial-selection system and decimating educational funding. He has often not told the truth, and instead of debating the issues he has engaged in character assassination of his critics.

He has acted as though any criticism of him is lese majesty. He is a bully. While he professes support for good government, his administration is replete with patronage appointments imposed on his commissioners.

Newsday columnist Bill Murphy wrote last week about the mayor's effort to sell municipal hospitals and his anger at Comptroller Alan Hevesi, who voiced his objection to the sale.

The mayor was quoted as saying, "People should understand that our public hospital system—while a wonderful concept and a good thing—very often is used by the politicians of this city as a jobs program for their favorites."

I nearly threw up upon reading that comment. Why? Because it's not the comptroller who has used HHC for patronage purposes—it's the mayor. Alan Hevesi has no access to HHC hiring—that's a mayoral fiefdom.

Giuliani's hypocrisy and use of patronage was reported by Joyce Purnick in her *New York Times* column of June 1, 1995. "'From the day that I started exploring running for mayor,'" Purnick quotes candidate Giuliani as having said in 1989, "'I have made it clear to every political leader almost from the first discussion we have that there will be no jobs or patronage—only decisions made on the merits.'"

"Maybe today, the mayor would amend his campaign quote to say that he would make decisions on the merits only after days of bad publicity, a near rebellion from the city's hospitals agency and indications that persistent press inquiries weren't going away."

Purnick continues:

"Because it took all of that to persuade Mr. Giuliani to kill his nomination of a politically connected candidate to run the Jacobi Medical Center in the Bronx. That candidate was Leonard R. Piccoli, ally and former top aide to State Senator Guy J. Velella, the Bronx Republican leader and one of the few Republicans currently enthusiastic about the Mayor. Mr. Piccoli was Mr. Velella's choice, and City Hall went along, even though Mr. Piccoli had to resign from the very same job nine years ago amid accusations of mismanagement."

Commissioners have been required to hire individuals whose names were given to them by the mayor or his erstwhile patronage dispenser, now Deputy Mayor, Randy Mastro.

On one occasion, a commissioner called me to complain about a hiring order and was on the verge of resigning. I cautioned against it until the job market improves. Other commissioners have similarly complained.

Last week, Giuliani posed with Mayor Willie Brown of San Francisco on the cover of *Newsweek* and was listed among the "25 Mayors To Watch." Giuliani must have loved this reference: "Want to see government reinventing itself? Take a look at the mayors in cities like New York and San Francisco.

But surely the mayor cringed when he read on. Professor Alan Altshuler of Harvard's Kennedy School of Government called him "probably the least lovable mayor New York has ever had."

Newsweek added: "Former Mayor Ed Koch has called him a horse's ass—and whom better to ask? Whether he's hounding a schools chancellor out of town, fighting Time Warner over cable-TV programming or berating the latest idiotic question at a press briefing—when he's lucky, he can get in all three before lunchtime—Giuliani delights in being confrontational."

After 23 years in elective public office, I've concluded that a good leader has to have the respect and admiration of those he or she leads. A great leader also earns their affection.

Giuliani earned my disenchantment because of his hubris and his desire to destroy people (Chancellor Ramon Cortines, Police Commissioner Bill Bratton, and Board of Education President Carol Gresser—to name a few) through personal attacks when they legitimately disagreed with him.

He believes in terrorizing those who exhibit independence or have opposing views on major city issues. He doesn't defend his positions with his arguments, but rather seeks to destroy a perceived opponent with invective. He uses this city's preeminent political office as a pulpit to bully and vilify those who criticize him.

What's my motivation in all this? Giuliani himself summed it up—better than I ever could—on Oct. 15, 1993. As the *Post* quoted him at the time: "The thing about Ed Koch that I think everyone realizes is that he loves New York, and that for him the best interests of New York are paramount.

He's right.

MAYORAL RACE SHAPES UP AS HOLD-YOUR-NOSE TIME

Unless something changes, the people of the City of New York won't have a truly first-rate candidate to vote for in the upcoming mayoral race.

Next Wednesday, the four announced Democratic candidates will get a chance to strut their stuff at a *New York Post*-sponsored debate. I know all four quite well. Here goes:

Ruth Messinger: When the Manhattan borough president was a City Council member, she opposed my administration and many of my initiatives. I characterized her then as a left-wing radical. When I now meet her for lunch, I generally tweek her.

On one occasion, after she had told me how similar our points of view are, I said, "Then why is it, Ruth, that when I think of you, I think of a young Bella Abzug?"

She replied, "You're wrong. I am very much like you philosophically."

I responded: "Then why is it, Ruth, that when I mention you, people say you remind them of a young Bella Abzug?"

Her comeback: "Because you tell them that I am."

On another occasion, I asked, "Are you still for commercial rent control?"

She responded, "I was never for it."

I said, "Ruth, how can you say that to me?—I was there."

She said, "I was for arbitration, not commercial rent control."

I asked, "You mean that someone else should tell the commercial landlord what rent he may charge?"

She answered, "I think we all learn and become better educated with the passage of time."

I have no doubt that Ruth is the most ideological of the four candidates. I also have no doubt that Ruth will bring into government the most competent people available to promote her ideology.

Fernando Ferrer: I've known Freddy Ferrer as a City Council member and as a Bronx borough president.

When I was mayor, I proposed, as part of my $5 billion housing program, the creation of affordable co-ops on a large vacant parcel of property in Riverdale. The local "richies" opposed the plan.

Borough President Ferrer became the Riverdale residents' chief defender. On the night of the Board of Estimate vote, I said, "Freddy, I need your vote."

He said, "I'm against it, Mr. Mayor."

I said, "Freddy, you're selling out your own people."

He said, "I don't believe it belongs on that site."

I said, "Freddy, if this plan to provide low income co-ops primarily to Hispanics in the South Bronx goes down, I will tell everyone in America you sold out your people."

He replied, "Who will believe you?" He voted no.

I've told this story many times; when I learned that Freddy was running for mayor, I repeated it on my radio program. Freddy called me and said, "Mayor, what you are saying is not accurate. May I come and see you?"

At the meeting he said, "You remember where you say if I don't vote for it, you will tell everyone in America that I sold out my people, and you add that I replied, 'Who will believe you?'"

Said I, "Freddy, that's what you said."

"No, mayor, what I said was, 'No one will believe you.'"

Baffled, I said, "So Freddy, if I now quote you as saying 'No one will believe you,' it's correct?"

He said, "Yes."

I only wish his mentor, Roberto Ramirez, the current assemblyman and county leader of the Bronx—who I supported against Mark Green in 1993 for public advocate— were running. He'd make a great mayor.

Al Sharpton: His talents include an ability to manipulate the media. And he demonstrated strength by getting more votes than Liz Holtzman in the 1992 Senate Democratic primary.

His disabilities include demagoguery, threatening behavior, anti-Semitic language, and the foolish behavior he displayed in espousing Tawana Brawley's false claims.

Also damning was his comment on whites doing business in Harlem in 1995, when he said: "We will not stand by and allow them to move this brother so that some white interloper can expand his business on 125th Street. We're asking our black community to go down there and do what is necessary to let them know we're not turning 125th Street back over to the outsiders."

He called me about a year ago to say that he had made a career choice, and that he was going to take the road of Jesse Jackson, not that of Minister Farrakhan. I wished him well.

But I don't think he has yet undone the damage he inflicted on race relations over the years.

Sal Albanese: Albanese was a councilman during my administration. Sal's problem is that he, like Ruth Messinger, is an ideologue on the radical left of the Democratic party.

His chief claim to fame is that he sponsored legislation—ultimately approved by the Council—that will require private contractors providing security, food, custodial or temporary/clerical services to the city to pay "prevailing wages" to their employees.

This effectively creates a minimum wage for the city that is near double that provided by federal law. The additional cost to the City is estimated at $15 million annually. Given the authority, he would do even more damage.

Rudy Giuliani: A thumbnail sketch cannot do him justice. He's a good administrator with a number of notable achievements—substantially reducing street crime, successfully taking on organized crime, standing up to the PBA in its efforts to do an end run around the city in Albany, and more.

Nevertheless, I can't support Rudy Giuliani in his efforts to gain a second term. There are a number of substantive areas where we disagree, two of the most important of which are his gutting of the merit judicial selection system, and his decimating education funding.

But foremost is his character. He is mean-spirited—he destroyed Schools Chancellor Ramon Cortines, Police Commissioner Bill Bratton and others simply because they disagreed with him.

He doesn't care that homeless children sleep on the floor without mattresses at the Bronx EAU. And he often does not tell the truth, even when he knows what the facts are.

David Dinkins' brief entry into the mayoral race made it a three-ring circus. His withdrawal now makes it a one-ring circus—but at least he's spared the ignominy and pain of a devastating defeat.

I will undoubtedly go through a lot of soul searching before November. I will, without question, vote for the person who I think can best govern our city.

But oh, how I wish I could be proud of my vote.

NEW YORK POST   JULY 18, 1997

WHAT HOPE FOR MESSINGER?

Is Ruth Messinger's campaign for mayor hopeless? When I ran for mayor in 1977, nearly everyone said my campaign was going nowhere. Some even suggested that I pack it in before the election.

Murray Kempton devoted an entire column to my pursuit of an apparently impossible dream. He wrote, "[Koch's] face is forgettable and his speeches not memorable," and said that while I was the best of those running, I should get out. I stayed and I won.

Can Ruth confound the pundits in '97? You bet, although the odds are even worse for her than they were for me. Abe Beame, running for re-election in '77, was tired and coming off of four years of financial mismanagement. Ruth is running against an incumbent who has a number of major positive achievements.

On the other hand, Rudy is a ruthless control freak who governs by imposing a state of terror on members of his administration and claiming credit for accomplishments he had nothing to do with, e.g., free MetroCard transfers. Critics are often silenced by his intimidating use of the mayoral bully pulpit to demean and punish. Nevertheless, Ruth has to face the fact that, notwithstanding Rudy's tactics and character failings, he has amassed a list of accomplishments that garner him huge support.

Yet so many of those—like myself—who plan to vote for him are in despair. I often ask people who are distressed with my criticism of Giuliani if they like him as a person. Overwhelmingly, they reply "No."

I ask, "Then why vote for him, if you don't think he is a nice guy?"

The response: "You can't be a good mayor and a nice guy."

Say I, "Really? Was I a good mayor?"

Universally the response is "Yes."

Then I inquire, "Was I a nice guy?"

Again, "Yes."

"Why," say I, "can't we have both?"

The response is, "Those days are over." I don't think they have to be.

What should Ruth do? She knows that Rudy will get the editorial endorsements of New York's four dailies. He has a 60 percent approval rating. My advice is to appeal directly to the voters. For example, she should seek an hour-long interview with an established TV reporter like Gabe Pressman to discuss her public record and convey what she would do if elected.

She should use Tony Blair's tactic and tell us how she would change the policies of the local Democratic party. Following are some of the measures she should advocate:

1. Pledge that as the city's economic situation improves, 50 percent of all revenue increases would be used every year to reduce taxes, both business and personal.

2. Request that the City Council adopt "Question Time" for the mayor to appear before it and respond to questions, as Great Britain's prime minister does before Parliament.

3. Restore the merit-based judicial selection system that Giuliani jettisoned.

4. Pledge to respond to all freedom of information requests (except those specifically barred by law) and not to require that the media and others sue to obtain information.

5. Support legislation to end the currently allowed preferences in government based on race, ethnicity and gender, substituting in their place other criteria—economic status, achievements in leadership, athletic ability, etc.

6. State she will continue Giuliani's policies on law enforcement.

7. Support the end of teacher tenure, replacing it with renewable three-to-five year contracts.

8. Pledge not to support the Reverend Al Sharpton if he wins the Democratic primary (unlikely as that is) because of his demagoguery over the years, including the Tawana Brawley matter. Require repentance and penance on his part before she ever endorses him.

9. Pledge to walk humbly in the sight of God and the people of this city if she wins. Unequivocally state that she will accept criticism and eliminate the prevailing climate of fear at City Hall—and mean it. Convey her understanding that if the people elect her as their mayor, it is the greatest gift they can give anyone.

10. Give us her vision for the City in the year 2000.

The first column I wrote after Rudy Giuliani's election appeared on the Sunday of his swearing-in. I wrote, "As Rudy Giuliani takes office, he has the support and good will of most New Yorkers." Two months later, I noted he had been tested by God (referring to snow storms) and the radicals (referring to Sharpton and an incident involving police response at a Nation of Islam mosque) and proved his valor.

In December 1994, I raised two disquieting issues: his incessant attacks on Chancellor Ramon Cortines and his needless squabbling with Speaker Peter Vallone. I inveighed, "Hubris is every mayor's greatest danger." In February 1995, I wrote, "What's happening to Rudy Giuliani?" adding, "I intend to support him in 1997 when he runs again. His achievements in a very short time have been remarkable."

How times change. Here we are a few months before the election and while I will vote for him, I cannot endorse him. In choosing between Giuliani's character and some of his policies and Messinger's sterling character but flawed policies and public record as Council member and borough president, there is no contest.

Giuliani has done a magnificent job in reducing crime. But his character flaws make it impossible for him to give credit to former police commissioner Bill Bratton, who put together the police team responsible for the initial successes, and to David Dinkins, whose legislation funded an additional 8,000 cops for the city.

A mayor must be able to accept criticism. He should govern not because of the fear he engenders, but because of the respect and affection his policies create. Giuliani's greatest character flaws are hubris and his desire to destroy those who are not sycophants.

My number one substantive difference with Rudy is his ending of the merit judicial selection system which was in effect for 16 years. Giuliani's reversal impacts the decisions of Family and Criminal Court judges.

These judges know their reappointment depends not on an evaluation of their entire record by the mayor's Judiciary Committee and the City Bar Association, but solely on the mayor's disagreement with or approval of particular decisions they made.

For many voters, this means nothing. I, knowing that the city is the largest litigant civilly and criminally in New York City, and that the courts protect us from arbitrary executive and legislative decisions, consider the issue vital.

I despair that the Democratic Party has fallen so low that it did not field candidates who inspire broad support. In 1993, a reporter asked me how I felt at the moment I endorsed Giuliani. I responded, "Ah, to be 68 and still relevant." My involvement is good for senior citizen morale. Why I'm involved was best summed up by Giuliani who said in 1993, "One thing about Ed Koch that I think everyone realizes is that he loves New York and that for him, the best interests of New York are paramount." He was right.

Will I weep if Giuliani is re-elected, or be joyous if Messinger wins? Neither. New York City will survive either scenario.

NEW YORK POST   **AUGUST 22, 1997**

RUDY'S DOING THE RIGHT THING

Each mayor fears a brutality case—and that some will exploit it

On Aug. 9, 1997 a terrible crime occurred in Brooklyn. Abner Louima, 33, a Haitian immigrant, was arrested by police officers of the 70th precinct, and taken to the precinct station house, where he alleges he was tortured. The first report of his abuse appeared in a column by Mike McAlary four days later.

Louima told McAlary, "They walked me over to the bathroom and closed the door. There were two cops. One said, 'You niggers have to learn to respect police officers.' The other one said, 'If you tell or make any noise, I will kill you,' Then one held me and the other one stuck the plunger up my behind. He pulled it out and shoved it in my mouth, broke my teeth and said, 'That's your s—t, nigger.'" Louima's recounting had the ring of truth and his injuries corroborated his story.

I thought back to August '89, when I was running for a fourth term as mayor and Yusuf Hawkins, a young black man, was murdered by white thugs in Bensonhurst, Brooklyn.

Every mayor of this city since Robert Wagner has feared a racial confrontation—particularly one involving cops—setting off a riot. Yet if the police are to do their duty and protect our citizens each mayor is obliged to make the following rebuttable presumption: If a cop is accused of brutality when making an arrest, the mayor must presume that the cop has engaged in the lawful use of appropriate force, unless circumstances are clearly to the contrary. Without this presumption, cops would turn away from arresting lawbreakers, many of whom claim brutality when none exists.

The racial killing of Yusuf Hawkins did not involve police officers, but because it came six weeks before the Democratic primary in which David Dinkins was my major opponent, many political observers concluded that I lost the election as a consequence of that terrible event.

At the time, the youth's father, Moses Stewart, told me that his son's death would be used by others to defeat me. I described our conversation at the funeral chapel in my book, *All The Best*:

> "I am so sorry," I said to Mr. Stewart, a black Muslim and a follower of Minster Louis Farrakhan, when I entered the room. He took me to view Yusuf's body. "So young, so terrible," I thought as I stood next to his coffin.
>
> "Mayor," Mr. Stewart said afterward, "I have been asked by the Reverend Jesse Jackson"—who had paid his respects to the family about a half-hour before—"to use Yusuf's death to help elect David Dinkins as mayor." He went on, "I told him I will not do that."
>
> I said to him, "Can I hug you?"
>
> "Of course," he answered.

A number of the principals involved then are still on the scene today. One is the Reverend Al Sharpton. In '89, he stoked the fires of hell and racial discord and led a march into Bensonhurst. I asked him not to because I believed it would exacerbate the situation.

As I reported in my book, I said, "While you have a right to march...you're not quieting the passion by marching into Bensonhurst. There is nothing wrong or illegal about a protest march. The question is, do you want to be helpful to reduce the tensions or do you want to escalate the tensions?...if you want to lower the passions, the thing to do is to find the people who committed the vile acts, make sure that their trials are expeditious, speedy, and that when and if the evidence is there, and they're convicted, they go to jail for a long period of time."

I was condemned for this statement in a *New York Times* editorial: "Mayor Edward Koch has always had a troubling propensity for sending the wrong message. He did that again..." A *Daily News* editorial said my remarks "sound like coded pandering to the basic instincts of some of [my] constituents."

In *All the Best*, I described the results: "The television pictures shown...confirmed my worst fears. As the 30 marchers, almost all of them black, walked through Bensonhurst, crowds of neighborhood residents lined the sidewalks, separated from the protesters by a thin line of police officers. 'Nigger go home!' was yelled again and again and again. Teenagers held watermelons over their heads as a symbolic insult to the marchers. It was so vile, so awful."

Mayor Giuliani has responded appropriately to the Louima incident, saying, "These charges are shocking to any decent human being, and they're being thoroughly investigated by the Police Department and the Brooklyn district attorney. These charges, if substantiated, should result in the severest penalties, including substantial terms of imprisonment and dismissal from the force."

The actions taken by Giuliani and Police Commissioner Safir led to the arrest of four police officers, including Justin Volpe and Charles Schwarz, who allegedly tortured Louima. More than a dozen officers on duty at the time are being investigated. Some had to have suspected what was going on. All who did and turned away are no different than the Nazi, Bosnian, Burandian, Haitian, Russian and other war criminals who tortured those in their custody or stood by without acting.

What will happen now? The demagogues are still out there. Some, for political reasons, will unfairly seek to hold the mayor responsible for the incident, as their counterparts sought to hold me responsible in the tragic case of Yusuf Hawkins.

I do not believe that this monstrous event will affect Mayor Giuliani's huge lead against any Democratic challenger. I am a severe critic of the mayor, but in this matter he is blameless.

Some will cite the comment said to have accompanied Louima's torture—"This is Giuliani time. This is not David Dinkins time anymore"—as evidence that Giuliani set a climate for the behavior of these police officers. That is grossly unjust. Giuliani has never countenanced or encouraged police misbehavior. He has been eminently successful in leading police efforts to reduce crime—which had been most rampant in minority areas. Now mothers in those communities can let their children on the streets without fearing they will be gunned down.

So far, all of the principals in the election have been responsible in their comments and actions. If Election Day arrives without another incident incited by the racists or the demagogues, we will have been witness to a miracle. I believe in miracles.

In the meanwhile, the mayor should welcome the U.S. Justice Department in to investigate this incident as well as other police precincts where there have been civil rights violations alleged.

New Yorkers know the police officers involved in corruption and brutality are not reflective of the vast majority of decent, courageous cops who risk their lives every day to protect the city from equal-opportunity criminal offenders. However, corrupt and brutal officers can no longer be described as a few bad apples; regrettably, their numbers are now significant.

Racism in all its forms remains the number one issue in the U.S. It's time for a new Kerner Commission.

NEW YORK POST   DECEMBER 26, 1997

WHOLE LHOTA HIJINKS GOIN' ON

Rudy looks awful in bus-ad flap & defense of his budget director

Before being re-elected, Rudy Giuliani had already displayed his mean-spirited nature. He showed that in his treatment of Schools Chancellor Raymond Cortines, whom he described as "whining," "precious," and playing the "little victim," and of Board of Education President Carol Gresser, when he said the issues were "beyond Carol Gresser's ability to carry on a substantive discussion."

Now that Mayor Giuliani has been elected to what under the law is his final term, he is under no constraints, and exhibits his hubris. I'm referring to two incidents since his re-election.

First was his battle against the ad that *New York* magazine put on the sides of MTA busses saying, "Possibly the only good thing in New York Rudy hasn't taken credit for." He should have laughed it off; instead, he took it as a personal insult and filed a lawsuit seeking to stop the ad. The U.S. District Court dismissed his complaint as it should have.

The mayor compounded his failings by using the corporation counsel to pursue the litigation. That has cost the city several hundred thousand dollars in salaries of city employees. If he believes he has a right—and I do not believe he does—to prevent the use of his name in the ad, then he ought to litigate the issue using his own lawyer and not cause the people of the City of New York to pay his legal bills.

The latest action illustrating Giuliani's out-of-control mode was his attempt to bankrupt the Citizens Budget Commission because it criticized him. He defended the action of his budget director, Joseph J. Lhota, who called the trustees of the Citizens Budget Commission and urged them not to support CBC's fund-raising dinner. That organization is one of the "watchdog" private sector agencies that monitors the operations of the city and, on occasion, criticizes the mayor and his commissioners for failing to provide services or prudently use the city's operational and capital budgets.

I believe that if President Clinton had done something similar through his budget director, there would be a special prosecutor appointed to look into it. State Comptroller Carl McCall believes that Mayor Giuliani has committed a crime that ought to be examined.

I don't know if it's criminal or not, but I know it's reprehensible. The mayor, ridiculously, has defended Lhota's actions as an exercise of the right of his freedom of speech under the First Amendment. The mayor has stood freedom of speech and the First Amendment on their heads in so arguing, because the government is prohibited from making any law abridging the right of free speech—and that includes intimidation by the government of its citizens with respect to their criticism of the government or of anyone else.

What Giuliani has done is threaten an organization's viability by threatening the people who fund it. All of these trustees and fund-raisers come from highly reputable security firms, banks, and real-estate developers who do business with the city. When they get a call from the budget director—and he could only have made the call if the mayor had authorized him to—does anyone doubt many will be intimidated since their very livelihoods may be in jeopardy? Lhota denies threatening those he called, giving several stories which, according to the *New York Times*, changed with the passage of time. The *Times* Reported, "Mr. Lhota respun his explanation."

What the mayor sought to do here is blatant intimidation of his critics. He's done it before. He regularly berates reporters who criticize him. He flays his own commissioners if they demonstrate their integrity by advocating a change in policies that shock their consciences.

I was a supporter of the mayor before he was elected in 1993, but if you criticize him in any respect, as I have, he sees you as an enemy, not as a critic. The *Post*, which has been his strongest supporter in the daily press—and even defended him on the *New York* magazine flap—nevertheless said of the latest action in an editorial, "City Hall has blown it big time this time." Lhota's telephone calls, said the *Post*, "are now threatening to deepen into scandal."

The *New York Times* said, "Since his re-election, Mayor Giuliani has sent the following messages: Officials will be protected if they withhold data from the public, or use their positions to get revenge on critics." The *Daily News* said, "So full of himself is the mayor that he cannot brook even the slightest criticism."

I don't doubt for one minute that the mayor can legitimately say that he's been criticized unfairly on occasion by the Citizens Budget Commission. Every prior-mayor said that, including me. It wouldn't have been wrong for the mayor to advise CBC that neither he nor his budget director would be participating in their kangaroo court, if he felt that way. That would have been OK, but it's reprehensible for him to seek to destroy the critic by cutting off its funding.

In my case, after the CBC had criticized me, unfairly I believed, Ray Horton, its director, invited me to be the keynote speaker at their dinner. I accepted:

In my speech I excoriated Horton, but with a touch of humor (which always appears missing from Giuliani's rejoinders).

That made sense to me. But you don't do as Giuliani has done, seek to destroy an organization that is a watchdog on behalf of he people by cutting off its funding. What the mayor did on this occasion is probably his worst excess to date from a good government point of view. It shows that he is no longer simply a control freak, but is himself out of control. He may believe and think nobody can hurt him because he will never run again for mayor as the result of term limitations. What he has done is a clear abuse of power. It illustrates the well-known maxim, all power corrupts.

Some have urged Lhota to resign. That is a senseless demand. In my judgment, Lhota never would have done it on his own. He did what his employer, the mayor, wanted him to do.

Despite Carl McCall's call for an investigation, I don't believe criminality is involved here. Hubris has not been made a criminal offense, and I don't think it should be.

Some ask why the mayor is so successful. They are referring to his recent re-election and high personal standing with the voters. That isn't difficult to explain. In the area of crime reduction, he deserves applause and support. That issue has been the number-one priority of citizens in New York City, as well as throughout the country. But priorities in the city are shifting to education and jobs. In the recent election, the mayor received votes from those, like myself, who were critical of him, yet saw Ruth Messinger as the candidate of the left wing of the Democratic Party seeking a comeback at City Hall. I did not want that, so I voted for Giuliani.

In a democracy with regularly scheduled elections, we can rely on another maxim: This, too, shall pass.

RUDY ATTACK ON COP PANEL HURTS

Every mayor lashes out at critics who make personal attacks on him. In response to insult I have said, "The mayor is not a punching bag," and punched back.

But I believe Rudy Giuliani's cruel and uncivil attack on the committee he appointed to examine the relationship between the city's residents and the NYPD in the wake of the Abner Louima case is a disgrace.

After seven months of hard work, the task force—working with members of the NYPD assigned by the mayor—issued a report with more than 100 recommendations. Instead of thanking the committee, the mayor held a press conference and dismissed the report out of hand. He derided it, referring to one minor recommendation, saying sarcastically: "So that's a good change. We can change it from affairs to relations."

His press secretary, underscoring the derisive tone, said, "The mayor was being sarcastic, not literal."

After an avalanche of public criticism, Giuliani has recanted. He told my colleague Stanley Crouch: "I made the mistake of giving the impression that the task force recommendations with which I agree—somewhere between 60% and 76%—were of no interest to me."

That's too late—the damage has been done. What a sad chapter for the mayor—and for the city.

When he was in real trouble in an election year, he called on a blue-ribbon committee of New Yorkers to recommend changes needed to deal with the Louima incident and other problems involving the NYPD. The mayor got accolades for the quality and diversity of his appointments to the task force. Everyone was an independent thinker.

Included were Bob McGuire, former police commissioner; Norman Siegel, head of the New York Civil Liberties Union; Dennis Walcott, president of the Urban League; Abe Foxman, director of the Anti-Defamation League; Stanley Crouch; Una Clarke, city councilwoman (D-Brooklyn); Guy Molinari, borough president of Staten Island, and many others. All were of the highest caliber and reputation.

The mayor needed such an independent committee to deflect personal responsibility for a police department unfairly charged as out of control by strident voices opposed to him in the election.

The task force did its best to address the issues, but he held its members up to ridicule, saying, "Some of the [recommendations] make very little sense."

Even those he may disagree with are not foolish, albeit perhaps impolitic. By any standard, the recommendations deserved the mayor's respectful consideration or thoughtful refutation where he disagreed.

The mayor's instant display of pique and denunciation can only embolden the aberrant brutal cop and inflame those New Yorkers who mistakenly see the NYPD as the enemy. His disdain increases the public's cynicism. The public will conclude it was all pretense on his part to tide him over until after the election.

Rudy Giuliani is a good mayor with many outstanding achievements, and that is why New Yorkers re-elected him. Regrettably, his personality is seriously flawed: He apparently believes he can do no wrong.

The message he conveys is that he and only he knows what's good for us.

Unfortunately, the mayor can't seem to help himself. He must lash out even when he injures himself.

The myth of the camel and the scorpion comes to mind. A scorpion by the side of the river asks a camel to carry him across the stream. The camel says, "Will you promise not to sting me?"

"I promise," says the scorpion and then climbs up on the camel, who starts to swim across the river. In the middle of the stream, the scorpion stings the camel, who in his death throes says to the scorpion, "But you promised not to, and now we shall both die."

The scorpion relies: "I did promise, and we will both die—but don't blame me. That is the nature of scorpions."

Fortunately, unlike the camel, New York will survive.

DAILY NEWS   APRIL 10, 1998

RUDY GAVELS DOWN ON JUDICIAL MERIT

In 1978, I issued an executive order creating New York City's first merit judicial selection system, ending the political selection of judges.

Under the City Charter, the mayor's appointing authority is absolute and requires no confirmation by the City Council. In contrast, the governor and President's judicial nominees must be confirmed, respectively, by the New York Senate and the U.S. Senate.

All mayors lambaste judges who they believe are soft on criminals, so it is vital that their criticism not chill the independence of the judiciary. Judges should make their decisions on the merits, not to please a mayor.

I pledged to reappoint every sitting judge whose term expired if he or she was recommended by both the mayor's judiciary committee and the City Bar Association. I pledged that any sitting judge who failed to receive the designation of both committees for reappointment would not be reappointed.

In 1995, Mayor Giuliani rejected the joint recommendation of the two panels and declined to reappoint two Criminal Court judges, saying his standards were higher than theirs. This ended my support of him for turning back the clock and gutting the reforms I had put in place. Many leading lawyers were unwilling to criticize the mayor, whose vindictiveness is well-known and feared. However, then-president of the City

Bar Association, Barbara Robinson, and New York State Chief Judge Judith Kaye did have the courage to denounce his violation of the protocol.

Now four years later, the *coup de grâce* has been given to the merit judicial selection system. Giuliani has rejected the City Bar Association's recommendation not to redesignate a sitting judge because of her lack of temperment.

He has now joined earlier mayors who excercised their absolute right of political patronage, appointing and reappointing judges at will. He joins Abe Beame, who in his last 30 days in office appointed 10 judges who had been found unqualified by the City Bar Association. Similarly, John Lindsay and Robert Wagner each appointed at least one person who had not received their own committees' approval as professionally qualified. In my 12 years as mayor and in David Dinkins' four years, neither of us ever violated the protocols.

If Mayor Giuliani believed in the merit judicial selection system—and the evidence is that he does not—then when he concluded the committees' recommendations were in error, he would have sought to persuade them to his point of view. Failing that, he should have maintained the protocols, which would protect the system for the future, by his example, from other mayors.

But that is not his style. He believes only he possesses the Holy Grail and we are all fortunate to have him making these decisions.

The City Bar Association, seemingly powerless in its battle with Giuliani, has implored him to reconsider, saying: "We think it most unfortunate that the mayor, in disagreeing with our conclusion regarding a particular judge, is departing from a 20-year agreement that has served New Yorkers well."

I believe the city bar panel and the members of the mayor's committee should resign in protest. Giuliani is doing incalculable harm to the independence of the judiciary, the institution that historically had protected the people from excesses of both the executive and legislative branches of government.

In 1995, when Giuliani began to dismantle the merit judicial system, the *New York Times* wrote, "Mayor Edward Koch voluntarily relinquished enormous patronage power when he created an independent panel to review judicial candidates....It was one of Mr. Koch's great achievements."

It was true four years ago and is even truer today. As Shakespeare's Cassius once asked: *On what meat doth this our Caesar feed that he is grown so great?*

RUDY'S CROWING DOESN'T MAKE THE SUN RISE

Mayor Giuliani deserves praise for his productivity agreement with the sanitation workers. However, the mayor mistakenly believes he started productivity, saying, "These are things the city attempted before and in the past wasn't able to achieve."

The first such productivity agreement with the sanitation union took place in my administration in 1981. We reduced the three-man truck to a two-man truck, saving $50,000 a year per truck with the city keeping $45,000 and $5,000 split between the two remaining workers—in 1998 true dollars a net saving to the city of $80 million a year. Will the mayor ever stop disparaging his predecessors when touting his achievements?

STEINBRENNER'S GAME IS HARDBALL

I have never pretended to be a baseball fan. As mayor, I dutifully attended both Yankees' and Met's opening days, staying for one or two innings and leaving my staff to enjoy the rest.

My lack of interest came about because my older brother Harold excelled at baseball and I stopped competing. I tell an apocryphal story about our mother saying, "Harold, you go and play baseball, Ed, you stay in the house and study to be mayor."

Now Mayor Giuliani wants to move the Yankees to the West Side of Manhattan at an estimated cost of $1 billion, much of it taxpayers' money.

Even I know that this is wrong and, in any event, not do-able. I'm not a baseball fan, but I do know about hardball politics.

Relocating the team to Manhattan is wrong because the Bronx Bombers belong in the Bronx; the city should be prepared to fund the rebuilding of Yankee Stadium right where it is.

And building a new stadium on the West Side is not do-able for environmental as well as cost reasons.

Remember Westway? Community and environmental groups stymied that worthy East Side highway project for years—and ultimately killed it through litigation.

There the environmentalists alleged that the rotted Hudson piers—which would have been removed to build Westway—were needed to help the striped bass propagate. I offered to build the fish a motel in Poughkeepsie to assist them in their assignations, but the federal court found for the fish.

The environmentalists were wrong about Westway. But they would be right to fight a proposal to build a stadium on the West Side.

It would cause massive traffic jams and sickening air pollution, insuring litigation for the next dozen years, long after the Yankees' current lease ends in 2002. The environmentalists would win that litigation.

Then there is George Steinbrenner. I know Steinbrenner. He is very engaging, but a ruthless businessman.

In 1987, the city and state thought that we had reached an agreement on a 30-year extension of Steinbrenner's Stadium contract when he asked for 90 days to make up his mind as to one of four payment options. We initialed a memorandum of understanding that would have given the Yankees luxury skyboxes and additional parking.

But Steinbrenner had not leveled with us. He negotiated a new cable contract of $500 million—and then told us he no longer would agree to an extension with the city, which would have required him to give the city 10% of the cable profits.

I believe Steinbrenner has no intention of negotiating a contract with the city now, and that he intends to move to New Jersey in 2002, after Rudy is out of office. In the meantime, he wants to give the illusion of negotiating so that fans do not abandon him and the team between now and their leaving.

What to do? The city should seek immediate, around-the-clock negotiations with Steinbrenner with the understanding that he state his intentions by a date certain.

Without that, Rudy is bargaining against himself. If negotiations fail, the city and state should consider financing or supporting a purchase of the Yankees. If a deal can't be made, the Yankees will end up not in Manhattan, but in the swamps of New Jersey.

Painful to New Yorkers, yes. But more painful to Steinbrenner, who would be remembered as is Walter O'Malley, who devastated Brooklyn by moving the Dodgers to L.A.

DAILY NEWS   MAY 22, 1998

RUDY RUNS CABBIES & CITY DOWN

Many taxi riders have horror stories about drivers who over-charge and drive dangerously, so cab drivers are an easy target for Mayor Giuliani.

But most cabbies do not deserve the scorn that has been heaped upon them. They work grueling hours. Normally, they safely and effectively carry 1 million passengers a day.

And the industry provides upward economic mobility for minorities and recent immigrants.

The Giuliani proposals would increase taxi operating costs, and drivers would become subject to license revocation—meaning loss of livelihood—more easily than today.

Yet when cabbies asked to meet with the mayor, he brushed aside their request, responding that there is "no negotiation." Last week, they peacefully protested by not operating their cabs for a day; the mayor responded by threatening to prohibit taxis from operating on future Tuesdays permanently. And he threatens, in the event of more traffic disruptions like yesterday's, the confiscation of more medallions, which are valued at $240,000.

If cabbies commit traffic offenses, fine them appropriately. But why won't Rudy meet with them? Why does he threaten them for exercising their constitutional right to protest peacefully?

An insight into the mayor's thinking is revealed by reading the speech he gave at his second inauguration. He said that freedom does not mean "people can do anything they want, be anything they can be. Freedom is about the willingness of every single human being to cede to lawful authority a great deal of discretion about what you do and how you do it."

The *New York Times* added: "In New York, he seemed to announce, that lawful authority was his."

Now-deposed President Suharto of Indonesia would have agreed with that philosophy, but many supporters of democracy are horrified. Must we really "cede to [Rudy] a great deal of discretion about what [we] do and how [we] do it?"

His threat to deprive taxi drivers of, on average, 20% of their income if they exercised their constitutional right to peacefully protest was appalling. Days later, realizing his gaffe, he announced in Chicago that he was only joking. I don't believe he was.

The editors of the *Daily News* publicly reported they had been told of the seriousness of the threat by the mayor's communications director, Cristyne Lategano, and press secretary Colleen Roche.

On another front, the mayor has begun a new battle, advising neighborhood residents to intimidate customers who patronize neighborhood adult shops whose right to do business is constitutionally protected, saying: "You know, one of the things you might want to do, which is perfectly legal, you can take pictures of people going in there. It really does cut down on business."

There is a discernible pattern in the mayor's comments. He believes that to question his proposals or request an opportunity to meet with him, or worse still, peacefully demonstrate in opposition to his policies, is lese majesty.

Public humiliation by photographing patrons of adult shops who are not violating the law is simply another illustration of his hubris. He is now the self-appointed arbiter of our viewing decisions, which goes along with his campaign to force us to be more civil.

But civility and Giuliani's own conduct are oxymoronic. The mayor reprehensibly is using his enormous power to intimidate all of us and is making New York City look like a hick town.

City Hall, for its occupants, has become a place of fear for the critic and the home of sycophants telling the mayor only what he wants to hear.

His image and place in history—notwithstanding his many positive accomplishments—are being tarnished by his own foolish actions.

COUNCIL RENDERS OUR KING RUDY HIS JUST DESERTS

Rudy Giuliani has two moral compasses. On the one hand, he is an honest man, fiscally incorruptible and fearless in the face of organized crime. On the other, he'll say almost anything to get his way.

In 1993 he asked me to support him against David Dinkins. I told him I could never support Dinkins for a second term after his sorry failure to stop the Crown Heights pogrom. But I was concerned about two incidents in Giuliani's prosecutorial career.

I said, "Rudy, why did you allow the federal agents to handcuff the stockbrokers in their offices? They weren't dangerous, so why were they humiliated before their colleagues by being taken out in cuffs?"

He replied, "I had nothing to do with that. It was the agent's decision because the brokers refused to leave, thinking the arrest was a joke."

Maybe. I asked, "How could you allow Sukhreet Gabel to tape her mother on the telephone to get evidence to prosecute her criminally?" Giuliani had been trying to prove that Bess Myerson, my cultural affairs commissioner, had arranged a fix with Judge Hortense Gabel to help Bess' boyfriend's divorce case. They were later acquitted.

Giuliani's response: "I didn't. I told her not to, but she inadvertently pressed the wrong button and taped her." He went on, "I explained this to the judge at the arraignment."

Maybe. The arraigning judge later told me such an explanation had never been made.

Rudy is now involved in a donnybrook with the City Council. Under the City Charter, the council is an equal branch of government. Under the leadership of Speaker Peter Vallone, the Council has overwhelmingly deferred to the mayor. Last week it did not, and adopted a budget without Giuliani's approval. Why? As the Roman Senate rose against Caligula, who planned to make his horse Incitatus a member of the Roman Senate, the Council decided our Caesar has grown too arrogant.

The mayor imperiously demanded an extension of the surtax on the city's income tax, which, by law, ends this year. This would violate the commitment made to the public when the surtax was imposed. Giuliani wants this and other taxes to pay the cost, upward of $1 billion, of relocating Yankee Stadium to Manhattan's West Side.

Contemptuously, Giuliani demanded that the speaker commit publicly to refraining from initiating a referendum—permitted by law—that would let the people decide whether taxpayer funds could be spent on the stadium.

George Steinbrenner, an arrogant bully, threatened to move the Yankees to New Jersey and blame the speaker if the Council required a referendum. Giuliani similarly threatened Vallone with blame. Giuliani and Steinbrenner denied collusion. Maybe.

I don't regret helping Giuliani defeat David Dinkins in 1993, or voting for his reelection in 1997. Choices must be made. But I no longer believe his denials concerning the incidents I raised with him.

I've concluded that when Giuliani was U.S. attorney, he acted as Inspector Javert of *Les Misérables*, for whom the end justified the means. Giuliani conducts himself as though he were the only competent and honest person left in New York City. He seems to think he's saving us as Joan of Arc saved France.

If he were right in proposing huge taxpayer subsidies to build a new Yankee Stadium in Manhattan, he would win the referendum. Apparently, he believes he would lose and intends to prevent the people from having their say. We are lucky Giuliani can't appoint members—or horses—to the Council.

DAILY NEWS   JUNE 26, 1998

HERE'S TO RUDY, A GREAT POLICE COMMISSIONER

Mayor Giuliani is battling the City Council, which lawfully adopted a budget without his agreement and then overrode his vetoes.

The mayor told Speaker Peter Vallone he would not accept any budget that didn't continue the income tax surcharge. That surcharge had been imposed to pay for 8,000 new cops with a promise it would end when regular revenues were adequate to assume the cost. According to figures from Doug Criscitello, director of the New York City Independent Budget Office, that day is here.

The newly adopted budget will end next year with a surplus of $843 million. Thus, the regular revenues are now more than adequate to pay for the additional cops. Nevertheless, the mayor now says he will not spend money for those items that he tried unsuccessfully to veto. One of the groups losing funds, the Legal Aid Society, told the *New York Times* that among those who would lose representation are elderly people whose benefits have been mistakenly cut off.

Why is the mayor so vexed? He wants to use tax money to provide George Steinbrenner, owner of the most profitable baseball team in both leagues, with up to a $1 billion subsidy to build a new stadium on the West Side of Manhattan. Most New Yorkers oppose this plan but support a reasonable subsidy to rebuild the present Stadium in the Bronx.

Believing he knows better than the public, and fearful of it, the mayor wants no input from New Yorkers, and he is successfully keeping a legally binding referendum on the subject—proposed by Vallone—off the ballot. Giuliani is doing that by putting a phony, unneeded City Charter referendum on the ballot, which by law would then bar any other referendum.

The mayor earlier admitted that there is no current need for Charter revision. Nevertheless, he is proceeding with Charter reform solely and crassly to preempt the Vallone referendum and get his way on moving Yankee Stadium to Manhattan.

The mayor—recognizing that he has little public support for his three current initiatives concerning Yankee Stadium, taxis, and food vendors—has announced a new initiative for which he deserves plaudits.

He wants to install controls on companies engaged in real estate construction, similar to the licensing provisions that he successfully imposed on the Fulton Fish Market, to end organized crime's stranglehold and use of cartels to drive up construction costs.

Such legislation exists in New Jersey and a few other states. When he moves intelligently and courageously, as he has when dealing with street and organized crime, the mayor is brilliant and to be admired.

Indeed, irrespective of how history will judge his eight years as mayor, it will certainly regard his eight years as police commissioner as superb. But he was elected to be mayor, who must be wise in his policies and appointments. Regrettably, too often in both areas, he has not done as well as he could, or as well as we hoped he would.

If there was one more foot to shoot, Rudy has done it again: the bunker. He sees himself not as mayor but as president, and the latter deserves a bunker. Rudy, however, does not deserve two—the current one at 1 Police Plaza and a new one at the World Trade Center—to call his very own.

The most trenchant comment that I have heard, and hear over and over again, is that this is one case where we expect the mayor to go down with the ship.

RUDY'S FIBER OPTICS ARE CROSSED

Last week, construction workers held a demonstration in midtown ending in riot, vandalism, traffic disruption, property destruction, and, most serious, injuries to 20 cops and three civilians.

According to the *New York Times*, the rally's "size and ferocity took city, police and even union leaders by surprise..."

It shouldn't have.

The *Daily News* tracked the demonstration hour by hour: "6 a.m. Thousands of construction workers begin to assemble...to protest contract to a nonunion New Jersey firm. 8:31 a.m. Police, concerned about safety, ask union leaders to shut down the demonstration. Police estimate the crowd at 40,000. 10 a.m. NYPD puts a call out for a Level 4 mobilization, the highest priority for officers to respond..."

What was Mayor Giuliani doing at this time? At 11 a.m., he was endorsing Attorney General Dennis Vacco on the steps of City Hall. At 11:30, he left for Nassau County to campaign with Vacco.

There is something amiss when the mayor leaves the city, in the middle of a riot, for partisan campaigning. If he were scheduled to be in, say, Washington to lobby for the city, he would have every right to weigh whether his presence was less important than his leaving town on city business

Responding to a New York 1 inquiry, I said: "I don't see any difference between what Mayor Giuliani did in not being present to control these 40,000 marchers who were out of control and who have engaged in violence and have assaulted some cops....He knows that and he leaves town. Why is that any different than David Dinkins, who stayed in Gracie Mansion when there was a riot in Crown Heights?"

Of course the Crown Heights riot in which Yankel Rosenbaum was killed and 80 Jews were assaulted because of their religion was far worse than this riot. But both mayors walked away from their responsibilities.

If Al Sharpton had led 40,000 followers into midtown, would the mayor have left town to campaign? I doubt it.

Also on a recent occasion, the mayor responded very differently to the taxi drivers who sought to demonstrate peacefully, preventing the demonstration with a huge police presence.

The mayor's recent bizarre actions on cabbies, food vendors, jaywalkers, street artists, and his bunker call into question whether his personal fiberoptics are crossed.

It's not enough to make the trains run on time. Common sense, compassion, and understanding one's own limitations must be part of a mayor's personality and character.

A Giuliani spokeswoman replied to my New York 1 remarks by saying: "Ed Koch is a sick, bitter, jealous former mayor whose craving for the spotlight causes him to lose sight of reality."

But the Giuliani shill's reaction to my comment proves once again the critical flaw in this administration and this mayor.

No mayor should believe he is above criticism—and this one does. On a previous occasion, he was more charitable in his comments, saying: "The thing about Ed Koch that I think everyone realizes is that he loves New York and that for him, the best interests of New York are paramount."

My current activities include: partner in the law firm of Robinson Silverman Pearce Aronsohn & Berman LLP, Daily News columnist, WABC radio commentator, Bloomberg TV commentator, "The People's Court," syndicated movie reviewer, adjunct professor at New York University.

Crave the spotlight? Me? Puh-leeze!

RUDY BEARS COP SCANDAL BLAME

Only two of New York City's last 11 mayors left reputations that include allegations of personal criminality. Jimmy Walker and William O'Dwyer both had to resign. Yet, in every administration, including those of honest mayors, there has been corruption, if only that of corrupt inspectors.

In some administrations, there were corrupt commissioners and other officials; and corruption in the Police Department is the constant worry of all mayors and police commissioners.

John Lindsay had the James Marcus scandal involving a multi-million-dollar, fraudulent city contract and a huge police corruption scandal. In the Lindsay era, the Knapp Commission reported that corruption throughout the department was systemic. Amnesty was given to many of the cops who had engaged in some criminal conduct, much of it petty, or the Police Department would have been devastated.

In my 12-year administration, there was the Parking Violations Bureau scandal, with corrupt contracts engineered by Queens Borough President Donald Manes and Bronx County leader Stanley Friedman, and a half-dozen other high-level officials in other agencies were indicted and convicted.

Mayors like John Lindsay, Abe Beame, myself, and, currently, Rudy Giuliani suffer the torments of hell when they learn of any corruption in their administrations. Indeed, for a brief time, I believe I went into a state of clinical depression. I thought to myself, "How could this have happened?"

While no one, including my political adversaries, ever charged that I was personally corrupt, as I noted in my book, *Citizen Koch*, I even contemplated suicide because of the shame I felt that it had happened on my watch.

Why am I reliving the facts and feelings that are still so painful? Because of the reaction of Mayor Giuliani to the current police scandal in his administration which so far involves about 20 cops and one sergeant who have been placed on modified duty. Some cops allegedly protected a bordello on W. 39th St. in exchange for free sex, and were turned in by a hooker to the Internal Affairs Bureau.

But Giuliani, instead of accepting responsibility, blames his predecessors. His initial response was, "This thing was going on for a decade and a half, and it was only the dogged efforts of the Police Department that uncovered it. And for all we know, but for all the increased emphasis on corruption in the Police Department, and the sophistication of the Police Department's new techniques, nobody would have discovered this."

The police commissioner, the cops in the precinct, and Internal Affairs are of course always responsible—as a result of the established chain of command—for taking so long to uncover the corruption. But as mayor for four years, Giuliani, whether he accepts it or not, bears the ultimate responsibility.

Moreover, Giuliani has even greater responsibility than other mayors because he has told us that he runs the Police Department. In every other mayoral administration, the department was run by the police commissioner, as it should be. But according to the *New York Times*, Giuliani even decides who should be promoted to detective.

He can't have it both ways. If he's running the department as he says he is, he gets both the credit and the blame.

Let me suggest that if cops are exacting sex for protection, there are other crimes afoot as well and in other precincts, of which there are 77. As the Roman Historian Horace said, *"Quis custodiat ipsos custodes?"*—Who is guarding the guards?

What we need is a restoration by the governor of the Office of Special Prosecutor with jurisdiction over the cops—an office regrettably terminated by Governor Mario Cuomo. The office's mere existence inhibited police corruption.

But at the very least, the mayor should implement the law creating the Independent Police Investigation and Audit Board, which would have subpoena power and the authority—independent of the Police Department—to investigate police corruption and brutality.

Why is Giuliani battling the implementation of this law in court? The Police Department cannot police itself.

RUDY MISSING WHEN THE ELDERLY NEEDED HIS HELP

Mayor Giuliani rushed to the scene of last week's 43rd Street construction disaster and took charge, holding a press conference to explain what happened when the 50-story outside elevator gave way, hurling debris everywhere.

The mayor met with representatives of the developer, the Durst Organization, and the construction manager, Tishman Construction, dealing with the financial problems of the area businesses.

Directly across from the accident site is the Woodstock Hotel. When I was mayor, I arranged the sale of the hotel on favorable terms to Project Find, an organization devoted to the care of handicapped and poverty-stricken elderly. The hotel became the residence of 275 elderly, one of whom, Thereza Feliconio, was killed when steel girders from the accident struck her room.

All the residents were forced to leave, in many cases without their medications. For the first 12 hours they sat in a hot, crowded room at the Times Square Hotel.

Then began the second tragedy, which moved me intensely.

By way of background, in 1987 I suffered a stroke. I was in a panic, thinking I would be paralyzed. No one seemed to understand that at that moment I needed comfort, not deference. I needed someone to reassure me.

Finally, one doctor, Sadat Hillel, who was giving me an MRI, said, after looking into my ashen face, "Don't worry, Eddie, you'll be all right; I will take care of you."

Such comfort wasn't afforded to those elderly people. One news article reported that when the developer and owner were contacted about taking responsibility for obtaining hotel rooms, they declined, until 12 hours later, to pay for the overnight rates of $125 to $180 per room.

Where were all the elected representatives? Two were there: Manhattan Democratic Council members Tom Duane and Ronnie Eldridge.

But the mayor did not come. This was the same day that the state announced it would provide a $24 million subsidy to keep one newspaper from relocating its printing plant to New Jersey; the same day that the mayor announced a fund was being set up by the developer and owner to compensate Times Square businesses for their financial losses.

Also, why weren't volunteers permitted for several days to rescue pets left behind in the hotel and other residential buildings?

Government exists to provide basic services to all and help those who cannot help themselves, particularly abused children and infirm elderly.

The Reverend Al Sharpton is often rightly criticized for his demagoguery, but he is supported by people in the black community because he is there with them immediately, demanding, threatening, pleading on their behalf if he believes they are not being fairly treated.

Why wasn't the mayor there on behalf of the dispossessed elderly and mentally ill?

A *New York Times* editorial was far too gentle itself when it said: "What was missing was the gentle treatment needed for those ousted from the Woodstock Hotel across the street from the tower...elderly and mentally ill residents were left for 12 or more hours without medicine and late into the night without housing."

Giuliani's presence was required. And he was only across the street.

RUDY CAN'T STOP HARLEM RALLY, JUST KEEP PEACE

Every year, the First Amendment, which protects every American's right to peacefully demonstrate, is under attack somewhere in our country. Most people will acknowledge their philosophical agreement with the concept until that concept is tested by an unpopular cause or personality.

For example, in 1977, the American Nazi Party sought a permit to march through a neighborhood of Holocaust survivors in Skokie, Illinois. Who stood up and defended the First Amendment rights of Nazis? The American Civil Liberties Union did. While I agreed the Nazis had the right to demonstrate, I said it wasn't necessary for others to join the court battle on their side. I was wrong. Courageously, ACLU leaders, knowing the consequences of losing many supporters, provided the legal representation that secured the Nazis the right to demonstrate peacefully.

Not long ago in New York City, Mayor Giuliani refused to allow taxi drivers to demonstrate. The mayor had to be overruled by a federal district court. The taxi drivers had been foolishly labeled by the police commissioner "taxi terrorists."

Now the mayor is faced by a more serious First Amendment situation. A former disciple of Minister Louis Farrakhan who has engaged in bigoted and inflammatory rhetoric against whites, Catholics, Jews, and homosexuals has requested permission to march on September 5th in Harlem, labeling his protest the

Million Youth March. He announced there will be gang members, including the Bloods and Crips, present from all over the U.S.

The mayor has said the march won't be permitted to take place in Harlem or on the proposed date. I understand the mayor's concern, but he's dead wrong on both counts. While the city can decide time, place and necessary restrictions in providing a permit, a court will decide whether the city's limitations are reasonable.

The mayor says the size of the expected crowd makes Malcolm X Boulevard (Lenox Avenue) inappropriate because of traffic requirements for emergency vehicles. Yet on September 7, Labor Day, more than one million members of the West Indian community will parade on Eastern Parkway, closing it for miles as they have for the last 20 years.

In deciding whether to grant a permit, government may not consider the content of the message or the character of the messenger. The activity must be peaceful. If there is violence, it's the obligation of the government to provide protection to all—marchers and onlookers.

The city has about 40,000 police officers—enough to insure compliance with the law. If this is insufficient, the mayor can ask the governor to have the National Guard stand by.

Khalid Muhammad, the Million Youth March organizer who harms black-white relations with his racist remarks, copies his mentor, Farrakhan. The latter, in less vulgar language, engages in the same bashing of whites, Jews, Catholics and gays.

What's indicative of the city's race relations progress is the immediate response of many black leaders, unlike their counterparts in 1985 when Farrakhan held his bully boy Madison Square Garden rally. Then, only David Dinkins and Hazel Dukes denounced him. Police Commissioner Ben Ward assigned additional police protection to Dinkins when Farrakhan denounced him to the Nation of Islam, exhorting the Madison Square Garden crowd, "He [David Dinkins] should pay a price....Do you think the leader should sell out and then live?"

Recognizing the need for racial, ethnic, and religious cooperation, Carl McCall, Charlie Rangel, and David Paterson, along with Schools Chancellor Rudy Crew, columnist Bob Herbert, E.R. Shipp, Sheryl McCarthy, and others early on denounced Khalid Muhammad and his message. The demagogues, black and white, think the good people of New York are in disarray. In fact, Muhammad is uniting us.

RUDY GAVE HATE MONGERS JUST WHAT THEY WANT

Mayor Giuliani and Police Commissioner Howard Safir snatched defeat from the jaws of victory Saturday at the rally led by Khalid Abdul Muhammad.

The rally, according to *Daily News* Columnist Jim Dwyer who was on the scene, drew 6,500 people—a far cry from even the reduced estimate of 50,000, the lowest turnout forecast by rally organizers.

A rally in Atlanta, organized by the NAACP and the Nation of Islam and held two days later, had only a few hundred in attendance. Both were failures.

Giuliani described the small Harlem crowd as a victory for him, saying his "strategy had worked."

What exactly was his strategy? Denying rally permits in violation of the First Amendment? Keeping the demagogue Muhammad in the news? Having riot police storm the generator at 4:01 p.m., just as Muhammad was concluding his speech—a speech that I believed to have been an incitement to riot and that should have resulted in a summons or arrest?

The black communities in New York and Atlanta overwhelmingly shunned the bigot Muhammad and deserve praise for doing so. In Atlanta, Jesse Jackson and NAACP President Kweisi Mfume implicitly renewed their "sacred covenant" with Louis Farrakhan and lost their moral authority by co-sponsoring the rally with the Nation of Islam and permitting Khalid Muhammad and his lieutenant Malik

Shabazz to join them on the platform and strut their stuff to the plaudits of the small crowd.

In New York, Giuliani and Safir failed us. They wanted a confrontation, and it appears they ordered an unnecessary police response, including a low-flying helicopter and police in riot gear moving in to disconnect the generator.

The initial police restraint in the face of disgraceful vocal provocation was in the great tradition of New York's Finest. But storming the generator was exactly what Muhammad wanted and led to a donnybrook, with bottles and chairs flying and 16 cops and some civilians injured.

The mayor said: "They had a court order. They had their free speech right. And at 4:01 it was over. And I am very proud of the police for making sure it was over."

If this had been a labor demonstration or one held by the Liberal Party, would the police commissioner have taken that action? Wouldn't it have made a lot more sense had a police officer simply informed Muhammad he had five or ten minutes to wrap up his rally and that he would then be issued a summons?

The results were predictable and to the mayor's liking. The police were used by Giuliani and Safir as if they are in banana republics.

Instead, the mayor should have thanked the black community for not supporting the rally and given it credit for the low attendance. But courtesy of Giuliani, Muhammad got what he wanted: martyrdom among some segments of the black community. The mayor fell into the trap of this racist, Jew-bashing, Catholic-bashing, gay-bashing bigot.

Giuliani simply can't help himself and exercise appropriate restraint when provoked by criticism, justifiable or not.

Every day, Giuliani and Safir give different reasons justifying the order that cops shut the event down. It is essential that there be a thorough investigation to ascertain what the facts are so as to properly assess blame and responsibility.

Manhattan District Attorney Robert Morgenthau has opened such an investigation. It would be appropriate for Bill Lee, acting chief of the Justice Department's Civil Rights Division, to undertake a parallel investigation to ascertain whether federal laws were broken.

It is also essential that if Khalid Muhammad incited a riot, he be prosecuted under federal or state law.

RUDY MUST TAKE A HIGHER ROAD IN DC37 SCANDAL

Since 1953, New York City has elected six mayors. Every one of them had at least one scandal of major proportions.

Mayor Robert Wagner had the urban-renewal scandal involving millions in city contracts. He was reelected because voters saw him as a good public servant. Then came John Lindsay, who with his slogan "He is fresh, and everyone else is tired," seemed to be just what we needed. His administration had the police corruption scandal and the Knapp Commission.

Lindsay was followed by former Comptroller Abe Beame, whose claim to fame was "he knew the buck." Except he didn't. The city's borrowing and financial condition were criticized by the Securities and Exchange Commission, and many investors were hurt. Beame was not reelected.

I like to think I was elected because the people knew I would confront the municipal unions and other special interests whose inflated financial demands were sinking the city. In my third term, I had the Parking Violations Bureau scandal. It happened on my watch, and I accepted political responsibility for it.

David Dinkins' major strength was thought to be his ability to calm racial tensions. His obituary will include the 1991 Crown Heights pogrom.

Rudy Giuliani was elected as a tough prosecutor to deal with crime. He has been very effective on street crime. Nevertheless, on his watch, we now see occurring one of the costliest crimes ever perpetrated in this city. It was perpetrated against the city's own workers and involved hundreds of millions of dollars in salary losses to them.

Worse, the city intends to enrich itself at their expense. It offered them a five-year contract, the first two years without salary increases. Stanley Hill, president of the largest union, District Council 37, agreed to the contract, subject to a membership vote.

We now see that the favorable vote was fraudulently achieved through ballot box stuffing, admitted to by two assistants to Hill, who has been forced to take a leave of absence. When the contract vote was announced, the presidents of two DC37 locals called it fraudulent. Their protest went uninvestigated by the city administration.

Mayor Giuliani now says, "It's a contract...they are going to find that legally they can't [undo it], no matter what happens with this investigation." Deputy Mayor Randy Levine, defending the administration's failure to investigate the original fraud charge, says, "It would be deemed an unfair labor practice if an employer became involved in an internal union matter like this."

Ridiculous. Where is the mayor's moral outrage? Where was the city's Department of Investigation? Who had the most to gain by the adoption of the contract? Who helped the two admitted conspirators stuff the ballot boxes? What were they promised, and by whom, to get them to take a criminal action that could subject them to years in jail? What did those in charge know, and when did they know it? We are fortunate that Manhattan District Attorney Robert Morgenthau is on the scene.

The mayor believes that other city unions, whose members did not vote and had terms of the DC37 contract imposed under pattern bargaining, are stuck with the fraudulently achieved contract. He is defending the indefensible.

DC37 and its 120,000 members cannot be bound by a contract that would have been voted down in an honest count. What should our advice be to a mayor who seeks to keep a fraudulent contract binding, when he chose not to investigate fraud allegations when they were first voiced? Rectify the fraud and provide justice!

NO MORE FACE TIME FOR 2 RUDY CRITICS

A reporter told me that Mayor Giuliani was removing two official portraits from the Blue Room at City Hall—mine and David Dinkins'.

The mayor's press secretary says the portraits are being taken out to be cleaned during the city's centennial celebration and will be returned to the Blue Room eventually—whatever that means.

But the reporter's information is that the portraits will be moved to the Governor's Room, a little-used museum that is rarely open to the public. The reporter asked for my comment.

I said, "There's a limited amount of room in the Blue room. It's his prerogative."

David Dinkins later said, "This mayor is apparently altering tradition. There's certainly limited space in the room, but if there's space for pictures of the city, then obviously there'd be space for the portraits."

Twenty years ago, under the direction of my then-chief of staff, Diane Coffey, the tradition of hanging portraits of the most recent mayors in the Blue Room was created. At that time, Robert Wagner's portrait was hanging in a corridor at City Hall. It was moved to the Blue Room, which is the most frequently used public room in City Hall and where the mayor holds daily press conferences.

When Abe Beame presented the city with his official portrait, Diane directed that the Beame and John Lindsay portraits also be hung in the Blue Room and that Vincent Impellitteri's portrait be hung in an adjacent corridor.

During my administration, we did move Wagner's portrait to the corridor outside the Blue Room due to lack of wall space—on the basis of first in, first out. When leaving office, I provided the city with my official portrait, which David Dinkins placed in the Blue Room.

I can only speculate as to why Giuliani decided to remove our two portraits. He has stated his displeasure with our critical comments regarding some of his actions and statements. He was particularly incensed when we issued critical joint statements. Perhaps having the faces of two mayoral critics staring at him from the walls of the Blue Room was more disconcerting than we could imagine.

Abe Beame, God bless him, is 92 years old without a furrow on his brow and not prone to caustic comment. Sadly, John Lindsay has medical problems; he quietly faces each day with enormous courage.

On reflection, David Dinkins and I are lucky that Giuliani didn't decide to cast our portraits onto a bonfire along with the First Amendment, which he seems to enjoy violating regularly with his denial of parade permits, demonstrations, and even the holding of press conferences (except now by City Council members) on City Hall's steps.

The entire building has been placed virtually off limits to the public, even though it is the seat of city government. Imagine if Congress closed the Capitol to visitors, something it has never done despite bombings and shootings.

Giuliani pleads the possibility of terrorist acts and has put police sharpshooters on the roof of City Hall, ringing the surrounding park with a 12-foot wire fence. City Hall today is reminiscent of the last days of the Roman Emperor Caligula.

I am nevertheless amused, knowing that what goes around, comes around. In my mind's eye, I see the next Democratic candidate for mayor emerging from the primary in 2001 and asking Dinkins and me for our endorsement. I also see us asking, "Where did you say you are going to hang Giuliani's portrait?"

RUDY'S VINDICTIVE— AND FOOLISH

I know something about the need to provide shelter for the homeless.

In my administration, we believed that using state armories as large shelters that could accommodate up to 1,000 people was preferable to creating many small shelters that would distribute the single homeless population throughout the city's residential communities. Despite the arguments of homeless advocates, shelters burden a community. And many of these people suffer from serious problems.

So I understand Mayor Giuliani's frustration on this issue. He was able to end the state regulation that restricted the number of beds in shelters to 200—only to have the City Council reimpose the limit by law. Nevertheless, his response is ridiculous, particularly when the Council is committed to "grandfathering"— that is, continuing the use of—existing shelters with more than 200 beds.

Without citing a need for more beds, the mayor announced he would punish Brooklyn Councilman Stephen DiBrienza, the prime sponsor of the legislation. How? By evicting a state mental health clinic in DiBrienza's district that serves 500 outpatients a day—the largest such facility in Brooklyn—and replacing it with a homeless shelter.

Giuliani tries to justify this by saying: "People who believe it is necessary to limit shelters to less than 200 [beds], I assume, are reflecting the views of their communities. It should be in those communities that the effect of this is felt, not the entire city."

This is the action of a petty and vindictive tyrant—and a foolish one at that. If there is one kind of facility that communities oppose more than homeless shelters, it is an outpatient treatment center for the mentally ill. So why uproot one only to have to replant it elsewhere?

What will happen to these poor souls when their treatment is interrupted and they have to travel to a new installation? Guess. Many will suffer relapses. And what of the neighborhoods where they will wander or live when they are no longer on their stabilizing drugs?

This is meanspiritedness writ very large. Even worse, it is dangerous, as evidenced by the terrible tragedy Sunday, when a mentally ill man pushed a young woman off a subway platform.

In his year-end interview with City Hall reporters, the mayor was angered when asked if it was fair to characterize his administration as "leaner and meaner." He replied: "I think that's an insulting question. Happy New Year. That's been a perception from the very beginning. It's something that you keep writing, and I really don't give a darn. I'm doing my job, I'm doing it as well as I can do it....If people like my personality, thank you. If you don't, I really don't care."

Let's examine his reply. Is there a normal person who doesn't care how others view him? If the mayor had said that if he had to choose between being respected and being liked, he would choose the former, no one could fault him. But he said, "I really don't care."

Yet he obviously cares enough to avoid the use of the word "damn," which apparently affronts some people, and substitute the word "darn." Does anyone believe "darn" is the word he uses in normal conversation?

So he does care. But he is so filled with himself and his power as mayor that he will seek to destroy an opponent, as perhaps he might have pulled the wings off a fly as a child.

The Council is not without recourse. Its control of the city budget is veto-proof. It decides what monies will be appropriated for mayoral agencies and mayoral staff. DiBrienza may be the subject of personal punishment. But does the mayor understand that as you sow, so shall you reap?

To Giuliani's "I don't give a darn," I say, "Oh, shoot."

RUDY'S RUDENESS COARSENS PEOPLE WORKING FOR HIM

Recently, I passed a hot dog store at the corner of Eighth Street and Sixth Avenue. In the window hangs a sign: "We are polite New Yorkers. Bravo, Mr. Mayor. We support your effort for a nicer New York."

The sign was put up about a year ago, supporting the mayor's crusade for civility. Regrettably, that crusade is occasionally at odds with the mayor's abuse of his critics.

As a rule, city employees should not engage in personal attacks on others unless they are acting in self-defense after being personally attacked. Elected officials have more leeway, but Mayor Giuliani's lack of civility has, by example, coarsened the comments of mayoral employees.

According to Giuliani, supporters of community gardens are stuck in "the era of Communism." Methadone users, he implies, are not "moral." Federal drug czar Gen. Barry McCaffrey is "a disaster," and a City Council member and advocate for the homeless is "a limousine liberal."

Giuliani dismisses anyone voicing opposition to receiving New York City's trash— including the governors of New Jersey and Virginia—as "some politician trying to get on television." He accuses New York City's Campaign Finance Board of "stubbornness and arrogance" and "the height of intellectual dishonesty." Between Giuliani and Campaign Finance Board Chairman the Rev. Joseph O'Hare, whom would you believe?

Finally, Giuliani stated that State Comptroller Carl McCall "has really no credibility." Yet the comptroller had by far the largest margin of victory of all the candidates who ran statewide last year.

Giuliani's incivility has infected those around him. Police Commissioner Howard Safir describes cab drivers as "taxi terrorists." Deputy Mayor Joseph Lhota calls those who reject Giuliani's plan to export garbage "pandering politicians."

Last week, when I attended Speaker Peter Vallone's State of the City address at City Hall, I detoured to the mayoral side of the building and asked the police officer on duty if I could view the Blue Room, which I had heard was beautifully restored.

He said not unless permission was obtained from the mayor's press secretary. I told him not to bother and not to feel bad about it, adding: "You're only doing your job. I'm going upstairs to the City Council."

At the conclusion of the Speaker's address, the press asked for my reaction and I said that the Speaker gave an excellent speech both in substance and delivery. Mary Gay Taylor of WCBS then asked if I had seen the Blue Room. I laughingly replied: "Well, I tried."

My response was reported the next morning along with the comments of Colleen Roche, the mayor's press secretary. She said: "The Blue Room, like the city, is in much better shape today than under former Mayor Koch. His jealously has become palpable, and he is obviously seeking attention."

I have no recollection of ever having met Ms. Roche, and I have certainly never criticized her. By encouraging mayoral employees with otherwise decent reputations to engage in scurrilous comments that denigrate citizens, the mayor demeans his office.

Roche also was quoted as saying: "If Koch had had a half second's worth of patience, the guard would have gotten somebody of the appropriate stature to meet him at the gate." Why would I need someone of "appropriate stature" to show me the Blue Room?

One reporter later suggested that if those really were her thoughts, it would have been appropriate for her or someone on behalf of the mayor to call and invite me to visit the Blue Room when they learned of the incident.

The mayor and his minions have coarsened discourse in this city. It's time to remove that poster from the hot dog store window.

PORN INDUSTRY LIVES, SO I WIN RUDY'S WAGER

A long time ago, I said ridding the city of adult establishments—which is part of every mayor's agenda, including Rudy Giuliani's—is more difficult than it should be. The porn beast is hydra-headed.

Back in July, with his usual hubris, Rudy told reporters, "Former Mayor Edward I. Koch once bet us that we would never win. He hasn't paid his bet yet."

At the time, I said I didn't remember such a bet, but if the mayor could produce "any credible evidence," I would be happy to pay it off. He hasn't. I went on to congratulate the mayor for his attack on X-rated businesses, saying, "I approve of exactly what he is doing here."

Regrettably, the beast is still with us. The *New York Times* reports the X-rated industry "remains very much alive and, in most cases, open for business." Hubris will get you every time.

* * * * *

Some people are shocked that Governor Pataki is seeking to punish the mayor for betraying him. How can Giuliani complain? The mayor outrageously and without shame seeks to punish City Councilman Stephen DiBrienza by situating a homeless shelter in his community. And he is trying to punish the Reverend Calvin Butts and the Harlem community by denying them economic development because of their opposition to him. If you live by the sword, you just may die by that sword.

DIALLO CASE EXPOSES RUDY'S FLAWS

Amadou Diallo's tragic death at the hands of four police officers and the still-unfolding aftermath are reminiscent of the death of Yusuf Hawkins 10 years ago, when I was Mayor. What is so interesting to me is how history repeats itself.

In 1989, I met Yusuf's father, Moses Stewart, at Yusuf's funeral in Brooklyn. Stewart was accompanied by the Reverend Al Sharpton and attorney Alton Maddox. Both Sharpton and Stewart told me that Jesse Jackson, who left shortly before I arrived, urged that Yusuf's death be used as the catalyst to elect David Dinkins over me in the primary six weeks away.

Stewart said he didn't want his son's death to be exploited that way but couldn't control this. Interestingly, both Sharpton and Maddox sought to protect me from the taunts of the black crowd gathered in front of the funeral parlor.

One aftermath is that Keith Mondello, who was one of the young men convicted in Yusuf's murder and who was recently released on parole, has met Stewart, a meeting arranged by Sharpton.

I felt sympathy for Mayor Giuliani—having been through a similar experience myself—at the rude way he was received at the service for Diallo in the mosque on 96th Street. Not by the imam, who was courteous, but by others, including the infamous Khalid Abdul Muhammad, former deputy to Minister Louis

Farrakhan.

At Yusuf's funeral, Farrakhan's bully-boys—the Fruit of Islam—provided security and kept Police Commissioner Ben Ward and me standing in the blazing summer sun for an extra half-hour rather than allowing us to enter the church.

Participating in Yusuf's service was Sharpton, then much more the rabble-rouser. Now, 10 years later at the Diallo service, there was the Reverend Al, trimmer in speech, girth and attire.

Giuliani understandably sought to meet with Diallo's parents at the service, but regrettably his overture was rejected. Too bad. That sort of thing fuels resentment on all sides and helps the demagogues like Khalid Muhammad.

The mayor wants to do what is right but apparently does not know how, and now he is paying the price for his mistakes. I often criticize his style. I agree with him on 80% of his substantive programs but disagree with him on 90% of his efforts at implementation. He believes those expressing opinions at odds with his are being "political." He is his own worst enemy, lecturing, hectoring and never listening.

He declines to meet his critics, one of whom—Manhattan Borough President Virginia Fields—is desperately trying to prevent a widening of the racial chasm. But the mayor's confidants have let it be known that before there can be a meeting, Fields must apologize for criticizing his plans to put Yankee Stadium on Manhattan's West Side.

When I appeared last week with Fields and a dozen black and white leaders who, appalled at the present state of affairs, urged restraint, the mayor disdainfully denounced our advice as—guess what?—"political."

Mr. Mayor, on the day of Amadou Diallo's service, I was invited to come to the mosque and meet his parents. I replied that for me to go at that moment would be seen by many as an incendiary act intended to embarass you. So I declined, suggesting instead a meeting at a later time. (It didn't happen because of the parents' subsequent return to Africa.)

Mr. Mayor, your inability to listen and your need to continually demonstrate your power to command and control is bringing you to the cusp of no return. My advice: Step back and listen to the voices of restraint from those in the communities whom you view as enemies.

These voices are, after all, part of the fabric of New York and entitled to be heard. The plea for justice from Amadou Diallo's parents is as powerful as was the plea for justice from the brother and mother of Yankel Rosenbaum, whose murder in Crown Heights helped elect you.

IF SHE DOES RUN, HILLARY CAN BEAT RUTHLESS RUDY

As the whole world now knows, Hillary Rodham Clinton is weighing a run for the Senate in New York. I hope she does it.

Will she run? Should she run? Would she win?

My answer to the first question is that I don't have a clue. My answers to the second and third are yes and yes.

In all likelihood, her Republican opponent will be Mayor Rudy Giuliani, who, because of term limits, has no place else to go.

For the past two weeks, he has been taking advantage of the public's interest in a Hillary campaign, riding her coattails into countless TV interviews.

Initially, he played an "aw, shucks" role, saying in so many words: "I don't know what I'll do and I won't comment on her until she enters the race." But after taking that line in his Katie Couric interview last week, he warmed up. Over the weekend he was on the attack, in particular denouncing Hillary's comment several months ago that she supported the establishment of a Palestinian state.

Among other things, he said it was unseemly for her to make any statement about issues between the Israeli government and the Palestinian Authority on which there is no agreement.

First, as everyone in America knows, I am a proud Jew—I wear the designation on my sleeve—and I support a demilitarized independent Palestinian state. In fact, according to the polls, a majority of Jews in Israel and the U.S. support an independent Palestinian state. Hillary is not out of the mainstream on this.

Second, on numerous occasions, Rudy and I and millions of American supporters of Israel have thundered, "Jerusalem must remain the undivided eternal capital of Israel."

Yet the status of Jerusalem is a negotiable issue under the Camp David, Madrid, Oslo and Wye peace accords. So Rudy is just pandering when he says Hillary shouldn't comment on unresolved issues.

If there is a low road available, trust him to walk it.

I have met Hillary only once, when I was invited by Charlie Rose to a gathering of those who had appeared on his evening television program. The gathering took place at the Regency Hotel, home of New York City's power breakfasts, and followed, as I recall, the final primary victory that insured Bill Clinton the Democratic nomination for President in 1992.

Hillary was there with Tipper Gore, whom I've known for years and could comfortably kiss on the cheek without appearing presumptuous.

Someone asked, "Do you know Hillary?" I said no and was asked if I would like to meet her. "Of course," I replied. Introduced to her, I said, sophomorically, "What do I call you, Hillary or Mrs. Clinton?"

In what I thought was a Lauren Bacall response, she answered, "Try Hillary."

I hope she'll run, but it won't be a cakewalk. She would be up against a ruthless adversary who is willing to play the demagogue if it helps his cause.

But on the other hand, in just three months Rudy's favorable rating has fallen from 60% percent to 44%. And this week, a *Time*/CNN poll shows Hillary outpolls Rudy in the city 68% to 28%. His neighbors know him.

If she runs, Hillary—like Bobby Kennedy—will be attacked as an outsider. But she will be a breath of fresh air.

It takes a state to elect a senator.

DAILY NEWS　　　　　**MARCH 26, 1999**

KEEP ON MEETING WITH YOUR CRITICS, MAYOR GIULIANI

On Wednesday, Mayor Giuliani finally met with Manhattan Borough President Virginia Fields. She is the city's highest-ranking black leader, but for more than a year the mayor had refused to meet with her. To protest this stonewalling and pressure the mayor into meeting with our civic leaders, I had planned to get arrested outside police headquarters on Monday.

As it turned out, I never got a chance to join State Comptroller Carl McCall and Bronx Borough President Fernando Ferrer there because a drop in my blood pressure sent me to the hospital. While recuperating, I received a get-well call from the mayor. I thanked him and offered some unsolicited advice:

Meet with Fields and allow her to bring the government officials and civic leaders she believes should be heard.

The Mayor told me he had already agreed to meet with Mrs. Fields at the request of City Council Speaker Vallone and would consider my other suggestion. Reaching out to a broad range of people is not only in his interest, it is vital for the city.

As organizer of the daily demonstrations about the Diallo killing, the Reverend Al Sharpton has conducted himself in a responsible manner. He cannot be ignored by the mayor.

Nor can the several hundred public officials, civic leaders, and concerned citizens who have been arrested for participating in a nonviolent civil disobedience campaign at Police headquarters.

While I was shocked at the handcuffing of former Mayor David Dinkins and Rep. Charles Rangel (D-Manhattan), I did not object to their arrest. This is the price you pay for civil disobedience.

But for many of those arrested, the goal is the indictment of the four police officers involved in the Amadou Diallo killing. This is not acceptable. The grand jury should make its decision based on the evidence, not on demonstrations or fear of mob action.

I have confidence that Bronx District Attorney Robert Johnson will conduct this investigation in a thorough and fair manner. If there is no indictment for state crimes, undoubtedly a federal grand jury will be convened, and the Diallo death, like that of Yankel Rosenbaum, will be investigated to determine if federal civil rights were violated.

In the meantime, the real issue is racism, and what the city can do about it.

The day I went into the hospital, Carl McCall called around 6 at night to say he had just been released from police custody with 140 others. Freddy Ferrer also called and said that while in jail, he and his cellmates felt a little like the Reverend Martin Luther King Jr. confined to the Birmingham, Alabama jail. But instead of sending letters, they were making cell phone calls.

Interestingly, to keep media intrusion to a minimum during my convalescence, the hospital suggested an alias for me, "John Callahan." I accepted this and thought to myself, whose problems will be solved sooner—ours or Northern Ireland's?

Everybody emotionally involved in the Diallo death has to step back and ask, "How do we—the most diverse and tolerant city in the world—deal with the cancer of racism in our society?"

Yelling past one another, making scapegoats of the vast majority of honest, professional police officers, is not the way.

Leadership is required, and at the moment Rudy Giuliani is our elected leader.

EPILOGUE

I hope you found the columns interesting.

My good friend and former press secretary George Arzt once told me that New York City's mayors are destroyed or seriously impaired by their perceived strengths rather than their weaknesses.

John Lindsay, who was mayor from 1966 to 1973, was initially hailed for bringing many good people into government who had never been there. Unfortunately, a significant number of these people were so erratic in their behavior that Lindsay's Administration was disparagingly referred to in the media as "fun city."

Former New York City Comptroller Abe Beame, touted as a financial expert, ran on the slogan "he knew the buck." Beame won, and served the City from 1974-1977. He is now remembered as having brought the City to the brink of bankruptcy.

My strengths were personal integrity and being a "hands-on administrator." Many people also said that I was the "quintessential New Yorker," which helps if you are the Mayor.

So when Queens Borough President Donald Manes (who was elected four times by voters in Queens) and Bronx Democratic County Leader Stanley Friedman (who was elected by enrolled Democrats in the Bronx and served as Deputy Mayor in the Beame Administration) were charged with corruption, people were shocked. Despite the fact that neither Manes nor Friedman were part of my administration, some people still could not understand how it was that I did not know in advance of their corrupt activities and did not prevent the wrongdoing.

David Dinkins, who had excellent relations with the Jewish community, was elected primarily because of a perception that he could calm the racial waters. Yet, the Crown Heights pogrom occurred in the fourth year of his term and he has been roundly criticized for his failure to stop it in a timely way.

Rudy Giuliani was elected because he was perceived as a highly effective law enforcement official. He deserves credit for the huge reduction in crime after his election. And, when Rudy's police were successfully cracking down on street criminals, he deservedly enjoyed immense public support. But when the NYPD—at his orders—targeted taxi drivers, street vendors, jaywalkers, dog walkers, and other groups of citizens, his support began to erode.

And when the Baez death was followed by the Louima abomination, and the latter was followed by the Diallo tragedy, many New Yorkers began to wonder if the NYPD was now out of control. They also wondered if Giuliani was responsible for the loss of control and the callous attitudes displayed by some officers. Had the NYPD been influenced by the authoritarian policies of a Mayor who had, for the most part, taken control of the NYPD, reduced the Police Commissioner's role, and announced that he "ran the police department?" The powerful, easily understood, and common sense political maxim "the fish stinks from the head" seems appropriate to the occasion.

Giuliani is smart and tough. Those qualities are necessary to run New York City successfully. However, Giuliani apparently lacks sensitivity to the needs of others. He made this clear when he said "If people like my personality, thank you. If you don't, I really don't care."

It will be interesting to see how New Yorkers respond if, as expected, Giuliani runs for the Senate in 2000. As U. S. Attorney for the Southern District and as Mayor, Giuliani's driven personality made him effective notwithstanding his nastiness. The question is whether he can have the same impact in the Senate.

As Senator Daniel Patrick Moynihan said when recently asked about the prospect of Giuliani replacing him after he retires, "You can't come to the Senate for group therapy. You need to learn how to work in groups before you arrive."

Time will tell whether Heraclitus, the Greek historian who 2,500 years ago said "character is fate," was timeless in his observation.

ACKNOWLEDGEMENTS

I have enjoyed being a columnist for both the *New York Post* and the *Daily News* which currently publishes my weekly columns every Friday. Over the last nearly ten years, I have written almost 500 columns, a small fraction of which on the Giuliani administration make up this book. I am grateful to both the *New York Post* and the *Daily News* for having authorized me to republish the columns that I wrote for them in this book form.

The book was put together with the help of my extraordinary staff, small in number, only three people. With their help, I have been able to write a weekly column, write weekly movie reviews and author a number of books, including this one and one that will be published next January, *I'm Not Done Yet: Remaining Relevant*, describing my ten years since leaving office at the end of 1989.

I want to thank my staff—Mary Garrigan, who has been with me since 1975 when she joined my Congressional staff; Jody Getman, who joined me in 1995; and Michael Landsman, the most recent arrival, who joined me in 1998. Howard Geary, a retired New York City Police Sergeant who was a member of my mayoral security staff and has been with me ever since; and, Joseph Ahern, also a retired New York City Police Sergeant, who joined my staff in 1993.

Over the last ten years, while my staff has been small in number, it has changed from time to time as members decided to pursue new careers. That staff included: Jonathan Cohen, Rosemarie Connors-McCallion, Mary Lehner-Maine, Rachel Schwartz, Kevin O'Connor, Tom Krane and Leo Duvall. They were all first rate.

I have always believed that if an individual is successful, it is because of that individual's supporting staff, so they have my gratitude.

About the author

Edward I. Koch served as New York City's 105th mayor from 1978 through 1989. He took office in the midst of the city's worst-ever fiscal crisis and proceeded to rescue the city from impending bankruptcy. Since leaving public office he has been a partner in the law firm Robinson Silverman Pearce Ahronson & Berman LLP, and has appeared as a commentator and critic for countless radio and television programs and newspapers. The *New York Times* called Mr. Koch "a media conglomerate." He has no intention of retiring from active professional life, ever.